John Lyle King

**Trouting on the Brulé River**

Or Summer-Wayfaring in the Northern Wilderness

John Lyle King

**Trouting on the Brulé River**
*Or Summer-Wayfaring in the Northern Wilderness*

ISBN/EAN: 9783337144227

Printed in Europe, USA, Canada, Australia, Japan

Cover: Foto ©Andreas Hilbeck / pixelio.de

More available books at **www.hansebooks.com**

# TROUTING

## ON THE

# BRULÉ RIVER,

OR

# SUMMER-WAYFARING

IN THE

NORTHERN WILDERNESS.

BY

JOHN LYLE KING.

"That innocent revelry in the luxuriance of summer life which only Anglers enjoy to the utmost."—BULWER LYTTON.

NEW YORK:
ORANGE JUDD COMPANY.
1880.

# PREFATORY AND PERSONAL.

The exhaustion that comes of the inordinate and exacting frets and activities of business, the languor and inertia of summer fervors, the *ennui* and satiety that follow the dissipations of social life, may find in the great wilderness retreats a grateful reprieve and a speedy reparation. When the haunts of game in the woods and the lairs of fish in the streams incite the passion for sport to couple itself with the quest and yearning for rest and vitalization, the wayfarer's pathway in the wilderness becomes a pilgrimage through abounding scenes of diversion and into a realm of fascination. The restraints and stress of civilization and the city, for the time, are exchanged for the exhilarating freedom and simplicity of nature. The respited sportsman, with only the rod or gun as the sceptre of his commanding will throughout the rude domain, gratifies himself and luxuriates alike in the footsteps of the advance and in the repose of the halt. He realizes in a fullness of meaning gained from happy experience, that, indeed, " there is a pleasure in the pathless woods."

The wildernesses of the North-West are free, vast franchises of gunning and fishing. The many rivers which vein these immense tracts with running waters, and the numberless lakes in recesses of the woods, are inexhaustible commons of piscary, of whose affluent stores whosoever will, may, without let, partake. For an excursion, and on a vacation furlough, to one of these streams noted for trout, three of the Chicago lawyers in August joined in a party. These were JAMES L. HIGH, author of the works on "Injunctions," "Extraordinary Legal Remedies," etc., JOSIAH H. BISSELL, compiler of "Bissell's Reports," and the writer, together with LORENZO PRATT, a Chicago capitalist.

The party sought recreation and mental rest. Other members of the bar had journeyed some of those regions, in their vacation freedom, on a tour of rest, sport and pleasure. They had found and reported a full and rare fruition of enjoyment, in their wanderings to and on the Brulé river. A like expedition, with identical purposes, following the path of Cook, Campbell, Judge Blodgett and others, promised equal and similar delight and good. It was a journey and sojourn in open air, made up of canoeing, tenting, portaging and roughing generally, with the incidents of shooting and fishing.

The outfit and supplies were provided in Chicago, and sent by the Chicago & North-Western railway to Section Eighteen, a station of that road eighteen miles beyond Marinette, Wisconsin. The other accessories—a team for the land route and the guides—were engaged in advance at Marinette, and met the party at Section Eighteen. The canoes were to be procured at Badwater, on the Menominee, where the water travel began.

The guides were Indians. One of them was George Kaquotash, a full-blooded Menominee, muscular, lithe, active—a veteran of the woods and of the Brulé. The other was Mitchell Thebault, mostly Menominee, with a French infusion of blood and name, with his complexion paled to a hue a little lighter than the usual Indian copper tint. Though with the manners and habits, in some degree, of civilized life, they were essentially, in nature and native dialect, Indians. In another August a second excursion to the Brulé river was made by the same Chicago party, excepting that Mr. FRANKLIN DENISON, also a Chicago lawyer, took the place of Mr. BISSELL.

This volume is an itinerary or narrative of these excursions. It is made up and revised from diaries whose notes were jotted down on the way. They were kept chiefly to vary or to fill up and divert idle intervals, or otherwise vacant leisures. The notes were off-hand, and took the impromptu form and pressure of the body of the time when pencilled. It was sought to retain and reflect to the writer, perchance to his fellow tourists, images of summer revels that might, in the light of memory, re-appear and vivify into their original charm and freshness. Their present publicity is more at the instance of others than at that of the writer himself.

They are now given to the press, in the trust that they may, in this form, prove acceptable to those who have sympathy with and interest in matters of forest and stream. Their merit is in their minute and faithful portrayal of the real life and adventures of real persons in pursuit of holiday pastime and respite. In the realism of delineation they may be serviceable, and so justify their reproduction, as faithfully revealing the really "jolly good time" that may easily, surely, inexpensively and quietly be had by any reasonable party exchanging briefly the toils of business for a temporary business of pleasure, and that in distances and with appliances within ordinary reach and possibility.

They may show how that business sped prosperously while the party was gliding in canoes, footing portages, dwelling in tents, sleeping balmily on hemlock couches, eating with eager appetite, and withal affiliating into a genial free-and-easy fraternity, knowing and having only that which was mirth-inspiring, health-helping, reposeful and invigorating. Of course, this is simply narration. And while angling was the main diversion and is the chief theme of its pages, the work is not that of an expert or proficient angler, who can speak by the card, or from a professed sportsman's point of view, or of one who can claim to discourse instructively on angling itself, or generally on its delights. Nor does it aim to be of the nature of a guide book or gazeteer.

"Though dear to him the angler's silent trade,
Through peaceful scenes in peacefulness pursued,"

the writer's experiences with the rod have been infrequent and not varied, and were those of an amateur and not of an adept. While he cannot discourse generally or didactically on this sport or the pleasure of angling, yet in portraying the real lights and shadows of a brief period with the rod, and somewhat with the gun, and the content, the cheer, the fruitions and happenings of a particular party of anglers while roughing it in the open air, he may indicate and illustrate some of that charm with which angling has always enamored so many persons of various pursuits, temperament and genius, and which has made it a devotion and practice of their lives.

Probably the secret of the infatuation of this amusement to most or many of the brothers of the angle, is to be found in the close and quiet communion and sympathy with nature essential to the pursuit of the spoil of the water. Sir Edward Bulwer Lytton avows that he can palliate the wanton destructiveness of angling by a consciousness that its pleasures have not come from the success of the treachery practised towards a poor little fish, " but rather from that innocent revelry in the luxuriance of summer life which only anglers enjoy to the utmost." Even that Dryasdust book-worm, the recluse of Oxford, Burton, has perceived a hint of this, and tells us in the "Anatomy of Melancholy" of angling, "it is still and quiet; and if so be the angler catch no fish, yet he hath a wholesome walk to the brook, pleasant shade by the sweet silver streams; he hath good air and sweet smells of fine fresh meadow flowers; he hears the melodious harmony of birds; he sees the swans, herons, ducks, water-horns, coots, etc., and many other fowl, with their brood, which he thinketh better than the noise of hounds or blast of horns, and all the sport that they can make."

It needs little experience on the stream to realize that this sympathy and converse with nature in her myriad forms of air, sky, woods, water, and the teeming life of bird and brute and fish, are a great part of the boundless delight of the "angler's silent trade." These mysterious influences and attractions of nature impart to the use of the rod a refinement and fascination which elevate it above the rank of a merely gross, illiberal, and vulgar sport. This is verified in the instances of many noted persons who, while swaying masterly sceptres over the minds of men, have yet also lovingly plied angling-rods in the secluded and quiet streams.

The recall of a few names will illustrate how

even genius has ennobled and accredited the silent and contemplative recreation. Many men of fame, even equal to Dr. Johnson's, have been eminent as anglers, and have redeemed and disculpated angling from his surly and foolish sneer. Gay, author of the "Fables," and of the "Beggar's Opera," must have fondly haunted and fished the stream and learned, while swaying a rod, what he has sung in his "Rural Sports." Who can say how much of the prelate and moralist Paley's speculations were meditated when he was seclusively and dearly trouting the streams of Cambridgeshire? He was, as Christopher North says, "a pellucid writer, and bloody angler—a ten-dozen-trout-a-day man."

We know that Sir Humphrey Davy worshipfully frequented trout-pools and salmon-streams with boyish delight, and captured their glittering spoil with rapture akin to that of a successful experiment in his laboratory, and that he prided himself, perhaps, more on his "Salmonia, or Days of Flyfishing," than he did on his invention of the safety-lamp. The hero of Trafalgar and the Nile, even after the loss of his right arm, wielded in his left hand an angling rod with a fervor and success akin to that with which he waved the sword of war and victory.

When Madame Malibran, a queen of song, felicitated Chantrey on his supposed *con amore* chiseling of the marble in his studio, the frank and modest sculptor ingenuously bespoke a ruling passion when he protested: "I'd rather be a-fishing!" And who that has read them has not hung with delight over the glowing pages of Christopher North, author of "*Noctes Ambrosianæ,*" and of numberless contributions to the literature of brook and loch, lake and river, that have idealized and poetized angling into a very nobility and glory of sport? Certainly, an amusement which in itself and in its accessories has unbended, diverted and charmed minds and men like these, must be far from gross, ignoble or puerile. It is not wonderful that in its pursuit many gentlemen sometimes, as Burton also observes, "voluntarily undertake that to satisfy their pleasure, which a poor man for a good stipend would scarce be hired to undergo."

Something needs to be said, generally, about the regions and waters mentioned in the following pages, the modes of reaching and utilizing them, as introductory to the accounts of the excursions thither. The river of trout, the Brulé or Bois Brulé, is a small, clear, cold, rocky stream of sixty miles, issuing from Lake Brulé, running south by east. Not far from its mouth it is joined by the Paint river, and their commingled waters flowing four or five miles, and then receiving another affluent, the Michigami river, as blended tributaries become thence the Menominee river. This is a tortuous stream of about one hundred and twenty-five miles, running into Green Bay, with the Michigan town of Menominee and the Wisconsin town of Marinette at its mouth. Both the Brulé and Menominee rivers are boundaries between the two states.

The Michigami river has its source in Lake Michigami, in the iron and copper regions of Lake Superior. Its course is southeasterly. Its length is about ninety miles. Our party struck this river at Republic, reaching there by rail from Chicago, and coursed it about fifty-three miles, making thence overland and water routes by Lake Mary, the Paint river, Mud lake, the Trout (known also as Sugar) river, Lone Grave (or Bass), lake and lakes Chicagon and Minnie, to the Brulé, a distance of thirty-five miles. With the exception of the Hamilton and Merryman lumbering company's camp, about eighteen miles above its mouth, the Michigami, from the point where the party touched it, traverses an unbroken wilderness. This can now be reached by team on a supply road from Badwater, which also extends to the headwaters of Ford river. The Michigami flows through the richest of forest scenery, and on its banks are numerous points where deer may be shot, and, at places where small streams come in, trout are found. Downward canoeing is a most delightful experience of the rambler on this stream.

The Brulé, formerly, also ran its whole course through a complete wilderness. It was then reached by overland route from Section Eighteen, on the Chicago and North-Western Railway, by way of Badwater, on the Menominee, and in canoes thence. Since that time, several changes are visible in the few lower miles of the river. About seventeen miles above its mouth at the Michigami, a dam has been erected, and there is said to be fine trouting at that point. A mile below that is Armstrong's Camp, and below the latter two miles is La Montaigne's Upper Camp; three miles further down is Cauldwell's farm, and five miles from the latter is Stephenson's Brulé farm. Here is the log cabin at which our party made a descent on the cook and his dog.

There is now a railroad, operated by the Chicago and North-Western company, the Menominee River Railroad, from the line of the former at Menominee River Junction to Quiniseck, about twenty-five miles. This point can be reached by rail from Chicago, direct, in about sixteen hours. From Quiniseck a new wagon road has been made to Twin Falls. Between the two falls it crosses the Menominee on a fine iron bridge recently constructed, and passes near the south end of Badwater (or Spread Eagle) lakes to the Commonwealth iron mines, thence north-easterly, near Fisher's lake, to Stephenson's farm, on the Brulé. From this farm supply roads run to points on Paint river, and also a supply road thence runs nine miles to Brulé dam, recently built. The distance from Quiniseck to this point is about thirty miles. This dam is a mile below Chickabiddy Camp.

Quiniseck is already something of a village, and is the depot of several productive iron regions. From Vulcan, on the Menominee River Railroad, a supply road runs to Sturgeon river, where both good hunting and fishing may be had. On Pine river, reached from Twin Falls, there are good fishing and hunting. From Carney, on the Chicago and North-Western Railway, a road runs due west, crossing the Menominee at the Peemenee farm of the N. Ludington Company, to the north branch of Pike river. From the farm, the road traverses a park-like and picturesque country of pine plains, Norway pines and scrub oak, and is reputed to be an extremely pleasant and easy route. The trouting on the north branch of the Pike, as well as on the main river, is said to be superior. Bass fishing and hunting on Caton lakes are very fine. There is a good hotel at Carney, where arrangements can be made in advance, for teams and supplies for parties in quest of hunting and fishing amusement at points and in regions accessible from that point. The sportsman may also make a fine trip on the Escanaba river, by reaching it by rail to Smith mine, and thence down the stream by canoe or boat to the mouth. Trouting and deer hunting on this river, afford most excellent sport.

In consequence of these recent openings up of mining and lumbering points, and of roads to them, the sporting realms of forest and stream are made more easily and directly accessible. A sufficiency or abundance of supplies, the necessary and proper staples of subsistence, may be obtained at the various logging and mining points. At Marinette and Menominee a retinue of Indian guides for a journey and sojourn in the woods, may always be had.

With the exception of the points now mentioned, the regions traversed by the Brulé and Michigami, are wholly a wilderness, unsettled, even by Indians. The only landmarks are the trails or portages, impassable except on foot, and known only to hunters, trappers, prospectors, locators, surveyors or adventurous sportsmen on summer rambles. There is no sort of habitation or cultivation. Not more than two or three parties, during a season, penetrate these forests. For such parties the supplies and appliances of subsistence must be taken along or obtained at the lumber camps, and must be such as will admit of being transported in canoes and packed over the carries.

The forests are almost impenetrable, from the dense luxuriant growth, undergrowth and fallen and decaying timber. There are trails or portages, as they are indifferently called, between different points, and these are passable only on foot, and most of them with difficulty in that way. The

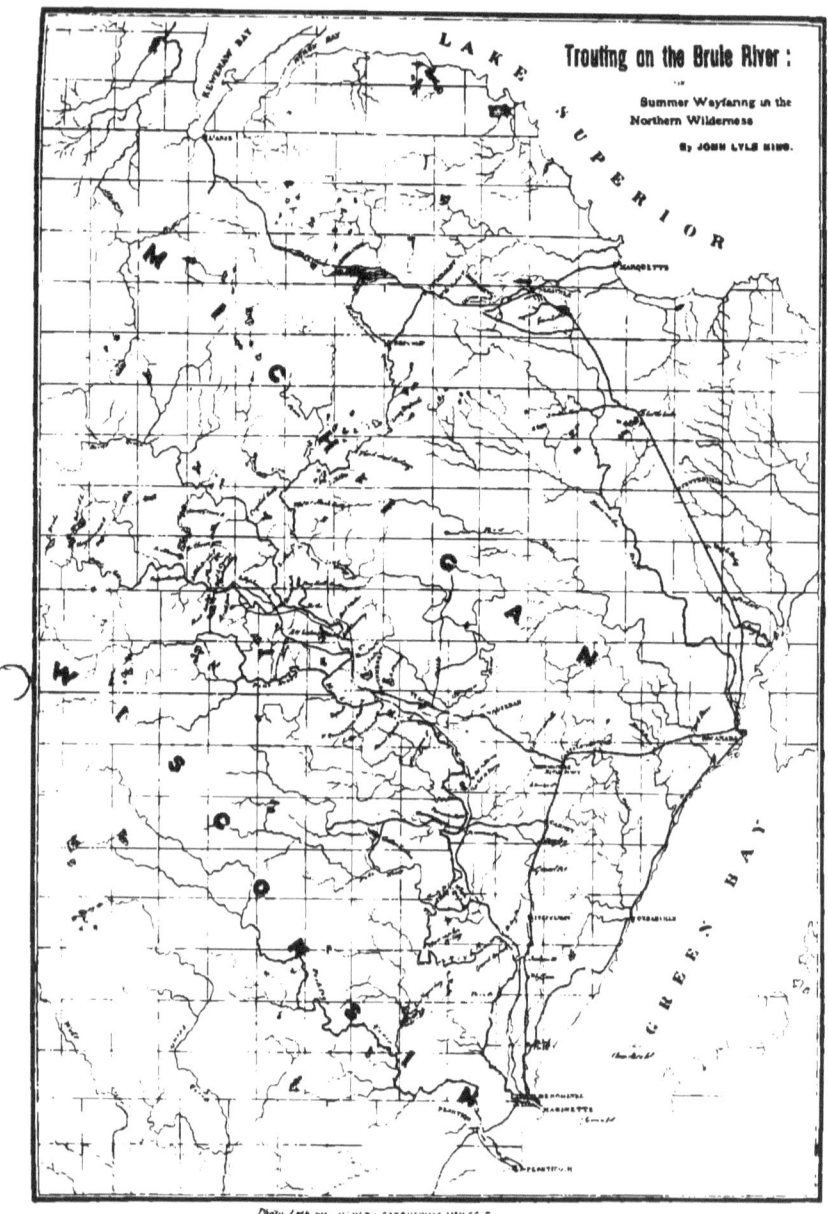

canoe is the means of travel. The country is threaded in many directions with watercourses, and interspersed with lakes and lakelets, and by portages, the canoes and the outfit of the parties can be transported from one navigating course to another.

In these regions mink, otter, deer, some bear, and waterfowl, particularly in their season, are found. The sportsman who ventures through the forests may find in them and along the water a surfeit of booty for his gun or rod. For the most part he is powerless, except when near some of the points within railway reach recently opened, to utilize the spoils any more than in supplying his camp fare as he passes along. Only in exceptional instances, and usually in limited quantity, his trout, or deer, or ducks, beyond the needs of traveling consumption, must be wasted or left behind, neither sufficing for his own prolonged wants or for gifts to friends at home.

As well as a canoe to move him, the traveler must have a tent to house him, and such outfit of camping appliances and such store of provisions as may suit his taste, his capacity of transporting them, the length of the route and the duration of his sojourn. Most essential, too, is the guide, his *cicerone*, the impersonated guide-book of the way, the navigator of the birch-bark, the carrier of the luggage, the tent-builder, the log-heap fireman, the cook, the baker, the scullion, in fact the indispensable general utility man and brother. He is, or should be, an Indian or half-breed, and practically they are the same.

He is a natural born forester. His nature, instincts, training, traditions, adapt and predestinate him to the vagrancy of the woods. The simplicity and paucity of his needs, his being a hunter by heredity, specially qualify him for the services and experiences incident to his position as guide. And though in contact with civilized life, and sometimes engaged in its industries, the aboriginal nature is only modified, but never wholly effaced by his habitancy and associations in town and village; and he still, like the fox, "ne'er so tamed, so cherished, will have a wild trick of his ancestors." His ancestry was forest-born and forest-roving, and by inheritance come his cunning and fitness in woodcraft and forestry. The white man, in these respects, only compares with him in proportion as he is Indianized.

The canoe and the redskin are the fitting complement of each other. Paddle-swinging and poling are necessary concomitants of his aboriginal and traditional utilization of barks of the trees for a vessel to float him, and for a tepee to shelter him. He is a canoeist by a sort of evolution of species. The tent, too, is a variety of his race habitaiton—the wigwam or tepee—the easily constructed and readily shifted housing and shelter of wanderers. His senses are acute and sleepless; of whatever pertains to the wilderness he will see and hear and scent and feel more keenly and quickly than those having eyes, ears, nostrils and perceptions schooled in the less exacting necessities of civilized life. These were our experiences of Indian guides, and they are confirmed by the similar realizations of other parties. This, of course, is the Indian of semi-civilization, of Wisconsin and Michigan, and not the war-whooping, scalp-lifting, thieving savage, "tattooed or woaded, clad in winter-skins," of the great out-West. We found him docile, patient, willing and zealous, and most satisfying in his service to us.

An excursion to and through the wilderness may, of course, be at such cost of time, of money and of such length of route as the parties may choose. The party itself may consist of any number of persons. The outfit may be of any desired extent, from that of enough, on a scale of frugality and moderation, to that of surperfluity, on a scale of elegance and luxury—either in a just comfortable or in a princely style. The considerations quite material in that respect are those relating to convenience, rapidity, facility and freedom of movement, and the smallest and least burdensome of *impedimenta* of course subserve or answer best those conditions.

The essentials of such a trip are simple and moderate. For apparel, a heavy suit worn on the per-son, dark shirts, changes of underclothing, and a few toilette articles, are sufficient. For provisions. a supply of staples, such as pork, flour, meal, potatoes, biscuit, coffee and tea, butter and lard, calculated on the scale of the army ration. A pair of heaviest blankets to each man and the tent are sufficient for the dormitory. With these must be the necessary utensils for cookery and a tin service for the table. To all of these may be added whatever fancy or taste may prompt, consistently with the portable capacity.

A party of four is probably the most pleasant and practicable for companionship and congeniality. The number of guides should equal that of the party. One canoe will transport four persons and half of the outfit, and that and the vessels can conveniently and without much strain, be carried over the portages. The expense of the trip will be proportioned, certainly, to its time, distance and kind of equipment.

A month's roving and sojourning in the wilderness, as distant as that of the Brulé, with ample outfit, not stinted of substantials for comfort, including the compensation of guides, and fare from Chicago and return, and the canoes, may be easily accomplished by each of a party of four, at a cost of from eighty to one hundred dollars. Those who have rambled in vacations in quest of rest, health and sport, in those or similar regions, have no occasion ever to regret their cost in time and money.

Since this work has been in type, the map and tables of routes and distances, have been prepared and appended. They were compiled from maps of surveys or other authentic sources, are accurate, and probably, as a whole, are the first that have appeared in any form accessible to the public. The distances stated in the book are such as were given by the Indians, or were conjectured by ourselves. The names of places are spelled as they were pronounced by the guides. In only a few instances are there errors of distance or of orthography, and they are trivial and unimportant. The map and tables will serve to correct them. For these tables and the map, and for other valuable information, the writer is indebted to Arthur T. Jones, of Marinette, whose intelligence in respect to the regions traversed, and their facilities for sport and modes of reaching them, is as conspicuous as the obliging and courteous nature which prompted him to contribute them.

If the lover of woods and waters shall, on perusal of this volume, be inspired with a desire to go and do likewise — should he perceive the charm and catch the spirit of idling, rambling and sporting in the wilderness—especially should the lawyer, wearied and spent in professional labor, seeking to escape it and the roar and whirl of the city, be led by the reading to betake himself, for needed recreation and respite, to the silence and peace of the great forests, and so refresh and vitalize his wasted forces for his renewed work of the desk or of the re-opened forum, then the writer's purpose has not been fruitless, his ambition will have been satisfied, and he may feel that he has in a sense not unmeaning and in a measure not unimportant, done something towards the discharge of that debt which Lord Bacon says every lawyer owes to his profession.

# TROUTING ON THE BRULÉ.

## CHAPTER I.

SECTION EIGHTEEN—THE START—THE ABORIGINES AND TEAMSTER—KAQUOTASH REFRACTORY—RAIN—RELAY HOUSE—A BOTTLE-FIEND—A CLERIC CURMUDGEON—ON THE WAY—ARMA VIRUMQUE CANO—FIRST BLOOD—GAIETY IN THE RAIN—AN INDIAN TATTERDEMALION—STEPHENSON'S.

AT two o'clock, afternoon, we shunted off, and dumped the outfit from the train, at Section 18. The eighteenness of the section was the most there was of it—that is, its being that distance in miles from Menominee. The rest—the odds and ends of it—was a small, rude, uncovered log platform, with a log cabin and a little wheezing steam sawmill in the background of a bit of clearing in the woods. Here began our acquaintance with the teamster, George Evanson, a tough Norwegian, with a span of rugged, stout horses, giving the most satisfying assurances of possibilities of draught in a wagon fit for roughing, and also with our aboriginal guides. The Indians were not the wild savages typified in the wooden effigy of the snuff and tobacco shops, with moccasins, leggings, blanket, eagle-plume and tomahawk, and with streaked and painted jaws. One was a full-blooded, copper-skinned Menominee, and the other a mixed-blooded Menominee. They were coated, trowsered and booted in backwoods attire. They were stalwart, and seemingly in superb order for our purposes. From their thews and sinews we had a prescience of splendid service and all requisite utilities. The first was George Kaquotash, and the other, Mitchell Thebault.

The road started rough and up and down. We footed some distance of the journey, to stretch our legs and straighten the crinkles of the railway sitting. Kaquotash was groggy. He seemed to fancy my company, and, in a warmth of spontaneous friendliness, vehemently fraternized me, and walked me hand-in-hand, until I tired of the grip. He proposed switching off and heading the team by a short cut through the woods. I declined taking a route of continuous shower-baths through the dripping foliage. Either from this, or because he was steaming up to fuller pressure from a nip he took from a flask, the fraternal affinity rapidly weakened, and he began to grow ugly, and soon, from mere "cussedness," or from a streak of untamed aboriginal deviltry, became impudent, defiant and mutinous. He threatened to turn back and go home. He sulked and grumbled. We halted in the rain, to appease him, or find what the trouble was. When our own patience was about exhausted at his perversity, he suddenly and unaccountably gave in and lapsed into sheepish quiet and servility. The procession moved on.

We had arranged our time-table to make Peemony farm for the night. The showers, however, rather abated the ardor of advance. The Relay House was eight miles from the railway. When we reached it, we were wet enough, with so many of the jolly kinks wilted out of us as to make us glad of a friendly shelter. Though it was but four o'clock and the fever of on-and-ahead was not all subsided, nobody remonstrated when it was cautiously hinted that the roof of a house was preferable to the roof of a showering sky, and, regarding the situation as inevitably determinative, we accepted the necessity with all possible good grace. Evanson unharnessed the dripping roadsters and stabled them.

We four moistly advanced on the bar-room stove, in which was quickly crackling the combustive fuel, and our wet clothes, when changed, were strung around to dry, and sent up plentiful steaming exhalations. George had an exclusive flask of whiskey, which he began to swig from, and which made him again ugly, noisy and very boozy. He muttered and mumbled unintelligibly at everything and everybody, and became an unmitigated nuisance. He was smart enough withal to embosom the fiery bottle flibbertigibbet under his red shirt, and there was no Chicago lawyer crafty enough to slip or steal it out. There was no help for it but to let his demonish familiar be exhausted to emptiness. It was sharp collective finessing to get him laid by for the night. As too inflammatory a ration for his native temperament, we determined out of abundant caution to suspend George from the franchise of the excursional grog thereafter.

After supper, we strolled over to the Menominee, a half-mile walk, for a glimpse of river scenery. It was narrow there, and brawled in little rapids. A short way down the bank was a large, abandoned, logman's cabin. There was a ghostly inmate within it, however, a Catholic priest with a lay follower, utilizing the gloomy hugeness of the hut for temporary camping. They were bound up the river deer-hunting.. It was evident that the consecrated sportsman loved to handle a weapon that was not spiritual, as well as to twiddle a rosary. He may have been saintly, too, but he certainly was not sociable, and gave us men of the world the cold shoulder. He extended to us, in no way, any benefit of clergy; and willingly suffered us to depart from him without fatherly benediction, or any implied *pax vobiscum*.

Next morning, we were egregiously chap-fallen when we took weather observations, and saw rain, signs of greater rain, and of rain all day. On, on, was the watchword, though the heavens should fall. A shower, after all, was a trifle, and must not be allowed to dash

"The even virtue of our enterprise,
Nor th' insuppressive mettle of our spirits."

George's whiskey-fiend was laid completely; he himself was straight, more white and less Indian, and in full feather with the party. We piled in the wagon and went on, heroically taking the drip as it came.

Pratt was our gunner. His weapon was a shotgun fowling piece, not brought for any premeditated service in the way of havoc to game, of wing or of foot, but merely as a usual and handy implement to have along, if anything should come in the way and permit itself to be shot at, and, at any rate, to help kill time with, if to kill nothing else. He was not a practiced marksman. We did not count much on his often harming bird or beast, and he himself was not very vain or conceited in the way of fatality or prowess with his gun. But for all that, he trusted in Providence, and in all the pitiless drench, kept his powder dry.

Though to any ardent son of saltpetre, the prospect for triggering was slim, to all appearances, a few miles out, three sick-looking partridges, soaked and bedraggled, spiritless as wet hens, poked stupidly out of a cover of brush by the wayside, flapped the raindrops off their wings and fluttered up to the limbs. This chance would animate a soul under the ribs of death, and aroused Pratt to the requirements of the exciting crisis. He uncovered his battery, so to say, and got out in the mud, adroitly stole a march to a good strategic point, made ready, took aim, and fired. An irrigated partridge "felt the fiery wound, fluttered in blood, and panting, beat the ground." The others of the flock were too weather-beaten and droopy to whir themselves far away. Pratt followed them up, and again sprung the trigger and let fly, but he let fly the miserable fowls as well, unharmed.

It rained steadily. We took the pouring without flinching. We had to. Hydropathic treatment was unavoidable. It was a great problem to keep the stores dry. We tried to tickle ourselves with mirth, and to weather it, or volatilize the exceeding moistness and ourselves with dry jokes. We jested at the rain, while it was pelting us. High had the face and ill-timed effrontery to torture us with his Arkansas hash story, a *variorum* edition of it, and so rung the changes on it as nearly to cause a manifestation of our Relay House hash. But in time the facetiæ became sickish and too flat. The heavy levity was too much for us. We relapsed into sullenness and sulks. We didn't care. We were resigned. We could join in Falstaff's invocation: "Let the sky rain potatoes; let it thunder to the tune of Green Sleeves, hail kissing comfits, and snow eringoes."

As we jogged on, the road worsened greatly. High and I, jostling on the seat with the driver, partially covered Bissell, Pratt and the tacit aborigines, who were astride and atop of the load, ballasting it, and to keep from being pitched off was all the art they knew. Rubber coats proved the wretched fallacy of caoutchouc. I wore one, which glistened in the most assuring semblance of imperviability, but my shoulders were no dryer than my legs. The water streamed off hats, and dribbled down our noses. We were soaked through and through.

The roughness of the road added greatly to the mishaps of the rain. The last ten miles of way towards Stephenson's were simply execrable. There was nowhere a level of more than a few rods. The vehicle canted from one side to the other, threatening to dump the top-heavy load of men and baggage in the ditch, creaking and straining, as in throes of trial, bouncing over corduroy, and pitching into holes and ruts. By way of variety of misery, some or all of us got out and walked, and soon, as we trod along, our boots or shoes were soaked like sponges, and squshed the water up our shins and knees. The asylum we longed for was Stephenson's, and on the *omne ignotum pro magnifico* principle, we idealized it into a blissful sanctuary of content and shelter. The only habitation between that and the Relay House was the Peemony farm, at the rapids.. The road trends to and touches the river.

At a deserted cabin a weather-bound, dismal Menominee tatterdemalion was crouching under its meagre vestige of clap-board roof for cover. Our natives interviewed him, and learned that he was navigating supplies up to Sturgeon river for John Stockton and Robert Clark, who were to travel the overland route there. This forlorn redskin was the solitary human being we yet had met all that day. It restored us to some degree of grim complacency to perceive that we were not the only, or even most miserable, sinners in such a woful, aqueous plight. Like the hares that went to drown themselves in a sheer desperation of misery, yet took heart to live when they saw the frogs in the pool, swelled to bursting with batrachian grief far exceeding their own, our hearts lifted from the depths, at the comforting thought that at least one wretched pagan was in more "doleful dumps" than we.

When told we were within two miles of Stephenson's our hearts rose higher from the depths. But it was a too flattering tale that hope told us. The buoyancy was premature. We did not know what that reputed two miles meant, either of distance, time, rain, road and travel under increased difficulties. Each mile, in the going, seemed a league, and the hour and a half of harder plodding thither seemed to stretch to three. After tugging slowly and crookedly up a hill, where the law of gravitation appeared to operate with more than its usual force against our ascent, the much-vaunted and eagerly looked-for Stephenson's hospice stood before us.

It was a large, double, low, pine log and logmen's cabin of the most primitive frontier order of architecture. But we promptly unloaded ourselves from the wagon, each one dripping like a bather from his wash. The wooden pile was a welcome castle of shelter. Interiorly, it was fitted up roughly but comfortably, for the needs of the hardy choppers, whose axes make annual havoc in the neighboring forests of pine. In one part, are tiers of bunks for sleepers, and in the other, are the kitchen and dining rooms. The loggers live there only in the winter; two or three persons were all who quartered there at this season.

We lost no time in changing wet for dry clothes. Every peg around the large stove was festooned, and three-legged stools were hung with an ill-favored display of drenched coats, saturated breeches, watered shirts and soaked socks, which so strung about, made the apartment look like a second-hand "old clo'" shop in Jewry. They were the cast-off *debris* of garmenture, then doing their last service.

Of all the Stephensonian denizens, the cook was the most important personage to us. He was a shiny-faced, stumpy young French Canadian, with a *patois* of Quebec and Boston. But he knew his business of skillet and dish, and discerning hunger as the one common facial expression of the crowd, he bustled around with promptness in preparing us a meal of pork, biscuit, potatoes and coffee. The spread gratifyingly surprised and satisfied us. At the signal we charged on the viands, and soon the bountiful provision vanished like the baseless fabric of a vision, scarce leaving crust or scrap behind.

There were signs of clearing in the sky, and the words "go ahead" were spoken; but then, that we were well dried and warmed, and could not surely forecast dryness and warmth for the rest of the day, we considerately resolved to wait, abide and bear the ills we had—mainly an impatience to be moving—rather than to chance others that we knew not of. And, as if specially to verify to us our sensible prescience in staying, it was not long before some western clouds trooped up in dark masses, and rained down like mad, and made us conscious of how wisely discerning were our prophetic souls, and how much the woodman's rude cabin was a friendly home of ease and comfort.

We had ample chance to overhaul the tackle and see to having everything in perfect trim. Bissell took the situation contentedly enough to spread himself on the floor, pillowed on a satchel, and in the glow of the firelight he reveled in the pages of Victor Hugo's "'93." High had a novel, too, and in it, apart and with his pipe, was wrapt in pensive contemplation, on a stool. Pratt and I cultivated good graces and friendly intimacy with the *maestro* of the kitchen bureau. The situation, for one of weather-bound confinement, was not, by any means, intolerable.

# CHAPTER II.

IN CLOVER—AFOOT—THE ROAD—STURGEON FARM—TO DICKEY'S—A LANDSCAPE AND RIVER VIEW—AT DICKEY'S—HIS DOG AND A DINNER—A CANOE—A HURDLE ROUTE—FIRST CAMP — BADWATER —TOM KING—EMBARKATION —MICHIGAMI FALLS—A PICKEREL CAPTURE—TRAIL TO BRULE FALLS—OLD SLEDGE AND NEW FRIENDS.

OUR host of the cabin meant us well, and was generous of his best hospitality. He had a couple of double bunks fitted expressly for our sleeping, and his choicest blankets laid to enfold us in their soft and ample spread. The arrangement looked well enough, and promising to our tired natures of sleep that would be balmy and restful. Yet when it came time to wrap the covers of the bunk around us, certain entomological speculations were aroused by the prying research of one of our observers, who had a restless habit of inquisitiveness, and more than a suspicion of the *cimex lectularius* crept into our study of imagination and perturbed us.

We were in a dilemma between considerations of vermin and of propriety. What to do or not to do, so as neither to offend our good host or our better selves, was a delicate question. But Bissell, in a pause of the rain, gadding around with a thirst for knowledge, or on a reconnoisance of curiosity, had discovered a haystack, a huge cone or mound of mown grass, with a movable roofing over it. He bethought himself of the haycock and imparted the discovery to us. We hailed this as a happy solution of the quandary. The haymow was moved as a substitute for the cabin scaffolds, and after the previous question, and then the main question being put — the party decidedly preferring the chance of hay-seed to a prospect of the hospitable bug—the matter was settled *nem. con.*

We stood not on the order of going. To charge on and scale the heights of the towering heap were no sooner said than done, and once on the summit, we were quickly cuddled in the blankets and nestling in slumbrous repose. All there is of being snug as a bug in a rug was each one's happy fate while snuggling in the haycock dormitory. We had at least stolen a march on the suspected lectularian pest, and instead of it, had nothing other than slumber "gently o'er us stealing." We fancied, however, that the master of the messuage greeted us with no very gushing morning salutation, when we crept out of the haystack. Possibly he felt that our giving a wide berth to his bunks was rather ungracious—a reflection on his accommodation and an insensibility to the kindness and hospitality meant in putting them into extra trim for our service.

The shiny-faced Canadian breakfasted us early for a timely start. A few minutes after five, before there was sun to glisten the drops on the herbage, we made our adieus to Stephenson's, and took to the road, which was exceedingly rough and uneven. At first we went afoot. But Pratt, who was slightly ailing, perched on the seat with the driver. When we mounted and squatted on the luggage, the bouncing motion of the wagon made it more unpleasant to hold the load and ourselves on than it was to walk. The choice between the vehicular and pedestrian mode of travel was about an even thing. We saw nothing but woods, passed two log clearings, heard a couple of unseen choppers hacking at invisible trees, went through a large sugar maple camp, and twice touched near enough the river to catch its silver glistening through the embowering verdure, and hear the babbling music of the rapids. Our natives went afoot, tramping short-cuts, and kept in the advance. Sturgeon farm was the first objective point, said to be fifteen miles from Stephenson's.

About ten o'clock we came to Sturgeon river, where it flows into the Menominee. Fording the former at its mouth—it being then from summer shrinking much down in the mouth—we struck the bounds of Sturgeon, otherwise New York farm, which lies there bordering the two streams. After the density of wilderness and naturalness we had traversed, it opened on us like a perspective of beauty and a scene of life. There are some good buildings of wood on the place, a capacious barn, a store-room, and a large acreage of meadow, the property of a lumbering company. It is the base of supplies and stores of various kinds, and also the abode of the choppers in the company's winter employ. There is an aspect of neatness, thrift, enterprise and prosperity about the farm. Its chief importance to us, however, was in its capability of supplying wants already felt. We were customers on its subsistence reserves.

The next point was Dickey's. Ten miles stretched between it and the farm. It was not a much more pleasing route than that already passed over. It led up a hill, and ran a goodly distance along a ridge of hills, and some of it was comparatively smooth going, while other portions of the road were rough and broken. We tested considerably our pedestrian capacities on the way. Huckleberries were plentiful, and we picked and mouthed our fill of them. There was much dead timber, with scattering numbers of skeleton pines and hemlocks, and nothing enlivening in the way of scenery to relieve the cheerless monotony.

We plodded wearily on till we reached a hill range overlooking the river. There was an open space from which the timber had been cleanly stripped, and a deserted cabin then in decay, was the sole vestige of a former busy logging camp. The ground was worthless for culture, but had a great apparent capacity for brambles and weeds. And when its original wealth of pines had been exhausted, the place was abandoned and relapsed into a dismal waste. But the site, desolate in itself, yet afforded an outlook of a charming stretch of river and forest panorama. The guides, with something of an eye for the beautiful, had told us of the view, and had led us to it.

High said that within his experience, which was one of considerable familiarity with the indigenes of Colorado, Utah and Wyoming, our Indian retinue were the first of the race whom he had known to have a sensibility to the charms of scenery. Kaquotash and Thebault lingered, as we did, in admiration of the vista. Below us was the river bending, a belt or outline of gleaming silver winding through masses of verdant forest magically coloring to varying and shifting hues, from the stirring of the breeze, the shading of a cloud or the full effulgence of the sun. The blending view of woodland and stream was much finer than that at Sturgeon farm, and was, really, our first vision of the Menominee picturesque.

We were tiring of the way, and longing for Dickey's, where we were to halt for rest and dining. The plodding along was wearisome, till the proportions of his cabin, in a patch of clearing, loomed into sight. Like the few and far between kindred structures of the woods, it was of the rude, primal, wooden style of architecture. It is a trading station, lonely in its isolation as a hermit's retreat, where the scattered few Indians repair to dicker their furs, skins and deer, for pork, flour, tobacco, gawdy trinkets and such commodities as suit their primitive wants and tastes.

Dickey, his cook and dog, were sole occupants of the solitary ranch. It serves as a domicile, as a store in a rudimentary form, and as a hostelry or inn, in a legal sense, as a place where the traveler is furnished with everything he wants, provided the traveler has occasion for very little. The little we wanted was a dinner. Our lean and hungry look was hint enough to the cook to vigorously bestir himself. We heard the clatter of pans and the simmer of the fry, and, in our waiting eagerness, grateful and tantalizing foretastes of the meal crept into our senses in savory wafts from the kitchen.

While the preparation was going on, some of us stretched on the bunks, or blanketed shelves, for ease. Dickey's white, shaggy dog jumped up and laid down beside the recumbent, or tried to; and when kicked out, betook himself to another and offered the same doggish familiarity, but with like result. The traveling of the day had sharply appetized us, so that the devastation of bread, pork, potatoes, syrup and Oolong, surprised, though satisfying, ourselves, but disquieted the host. Probably, with limited supplies in the out-of-the-way cabin, the exploits of our six able-bodied appetites in reducing his stores, might easily have inspired some anxiety, if not actual consternation. But we were traveling in search of appetites of zest and longing unknown to the lagging or dormant appetence of the home-stomach.

It was here that I gave way to the seductiveness of tobacco. I had long been a cloud-compeller, but for the two years previously was a teetotaler in smoking, and the delicious aroma of the weed was only known to me in the vain fruition of occasional collateral sweets and sideway perfumes, which chanced to be whiffed about by other smokers. But here, looking forward to days and nights in the woods, where, of all places, my ancient familiar or genius of the fume, would be an always readily evoked and answering solace and companion, alike in the hours of the sun and of the stars, and when just at my side I saw High leaning against a tree puffing so pleasingly, and as if impersonating all the beatitudes, and the rich burning incense that spread in a glory of cloud and odor from his amber-tipped and ruddy-tinted meerschaum—"O, it came in my nose like the sweet scent that breathes upon a bank of violets, stealing and giving odor"—the smoking passion sprang from its trance of two years like smouldered embers leaping into instant, living flame.

I was at once irrecoverably enthralled in the delicious spell, and felt my utter impotency to banish the fascinating Satan-tempter to the rear. I threw myself headlong, as it were, into the full tide of fruition. Dickey had clay-pipes and yellow paper packages of tobacco with the Milwaukee trade-mark on. Of these I provided a supply; as they were the best in Dickey's bazaar, I was not inclined to be critical or squeamish. The luxury of that first after-dinner smoking was a supreme felicity indeed.

"And the last trace of feeling with life shall depart,
Ere the smoke of that moment shall pass from my heart."

Our prospectus of the journey had noted on it, "canoes at Badwater." But Dickey's saleable estate included a birch bark. It occurring to us that as a bird in the hand is worth more than the possible or uncertain bird or dozen birds in the bush, a canoe we could secure was more valuable and to our purpose than supposed or conjectural canoes up the river, we advised ourselves to invest in a present vessel. Our marine force, George and Thebault, was dispatched to the river to inspect the offered bargain and report. We put the matter in our pipes and leisurely smoked it while they were gone. Their report was satisfactory. The canoe was first-class, and ready for instant service. Dickey's figure was twenty dollars. The score was settled.

The Indians returned to the river, and soon thence shouldered the vessel to us, when we saw at a glance that we had acquired a very model and beauty of water-craft. It had dimensions for storage. It was staunch and tight; it was graceful and shapely; and when George lifted and balanced it on his head, to carry it through the woods, we saw its good qualities of form, size, grace and portability, at a glance. It protruded like an elongated, but seemingly imponderable, hood of bark, or huge fibrous pod. Nothing but Indian experience and patience could have worked it a way through such woods. High went afoot with it and the natives. It was to be portaged to a point above Twin Falls. On the trail were two small lakes. Bissell, Pratt and myself went with the wagon.

The route, or landway, from Dickey's to Badwater was ten miles. It was not really a road, in the sense of that leveling, grubbing, filling and cutting, which are supposed to be implied in the legal conception of a road where there are supervisors of highways about. The ground was of varying grades and forms of curve; declivities and acclivities, on spurs of little hills, seemingly too abrupt for safe teaming, and menacing constant upsettings. The branches of trees had often to be pushed aside;

they scratched into the driver's eyes, and if our Norwegian Jehu had been long-haired, like his remote barbarous Norse progenitors, there were many obtrusive limbs which might have swung him, like Absalom, by the locks. The trail was sometimes blocked with fallen trees, and the barricade yielded only to the axe, or it might be, trees had to be felled to open a detour.

One of us went afoot, in advance, to explore the way. Another followed behind to see that nothing slipped or jarred out of the wagon. We skirted one of the lakelets which the Indians had crossed with the canoe, and soon after, coming to another sheet, a perilous looking bog or slough extended across the way, and there was nothing for us but to risk the treacherous passage. The horses plunged in the slough, and at once sank to their bellies, and pitched forward and fell, one nearly on top of the other. They floundered and struggled a moment. The teamster waded in, and rapidly unharnessing the animals, they recovered their legs, and being hitched to the tongue and put to their mettle, after sundry hard pulls, they jerked the vehicle from the mire, out on solid ground. We were in not a little suspense as to the probability of extricating the wagon, in its integrity, from the awkward fix.

When the route touched the river above Twin Falls, Pratt left the team and navigated with High the canoe there launched and awaiting him. There were then five miles of roughing before us. In that distance, there were the same, or more, obstacles to impede our journeying. Fortunately, the horses were of the sturdy and enduring kind. Their day's work would have worn down common scrubs. Evanson was an experienced teamster, and knew his business well. So neither wagon nor horses had any but trivial mishaps, though it was almost a miracle that we had not been capsized a dozen times. Towards the close of the day and the end of the route, difficulties provokingly multiplied. The timber across the trail appeared to be larger and plentier, and the chopping was more laborious.

The gloom of the twilight gathered in the trees above us, and before we had made way to the end of the trail, the night encompassed us in darkness; the twinkle of the stars through the overshadowing foliage was too feeble a glimmer to guide us among the mazes. We groped the way cautiously, and, spite of his skill in night-driving, the teamster drove much at hap-hazard, or trusted to his horses. When within a few rods of the intended stopping place, we were impeded in a fastness of fallen timber from which there was no getting on or going back. We were unwittingly impounded for the night. We were actually nearer the river than we supposed, as in a moment or so, we heard the halloo signal of the water-wayfarers, who had themselves but just barely escaped the fate of being helplessly benighted down the river. Our responding shouts brought them quickly to us.

As we had to make the best of the imbroglio in which we had insnared ourselves, an available spot for camping was found by candle light. It was short work to heap and fire a log pile into flames. With the increasing irradiation of the blazes, the dark shadows of the woods lighted up, and the foliage changed into weird shapes as the glare of the firelight illumined and wavered. They lent us, too, a glow of good cheer. We could well have resigned ourselves to the situation, were it not that the same camp-fire which brightened us was the signal for the mosquitoes to swarm upon us for an eager reception.

So too, those winged motes, with most annoying perforating effects, the midgets, unmercifully pricked us at every exposure of cuticle. Even the oil and tar with which we smeared our faces, necks and hands, gave little protection against the stinging pests. But neither they nor the abundant viands of Dickey's dinner, abated our eagerness for another meal. Thebault's first exploit with kettle and pan, though rather hurried, so as sooner to meet the vehemency of our demands, was impatiently awaited. We came up smiling to our first table, the provision box, with blanket bundles for seats, and we unanimously pronounced the supper a happy success.

We too readily yielded to sleep to be long or much worried by mosquitoes and midgets. In the tent, though, the notes of their morning reveille were early and vigorously struck, and there was but slight yearning for a little more slumber and folding of the hands in the blanket couch. The surroundings were not pleasant, and we were not loth to be off on the way. The matinal repast was speeded and despatched with, at least, the reputed American devouring haste. We set our shoulders to the wheel (figuratively) and helped the wagon out of its nocturnal dead-lock. In daylight, it could scarcely have been driven purposely into such an environment of timber. Evanson left us for his solitary return journey, with many parting good wishes. We then lost no time in moving ourselves and the expeditionary paraphernalia to the river bank.

Small meadows on either side, with five or six rude Indian cabins scattered over them, all but one on the Michigan shore, were the vista before us, called Badwater. A squalid Chippewa, with a few ragged redskin youngsters, were the populace that silently and curiously hung around. Across was Tom King's cabin home. This name was an adopted *alias.* He was really, and of his race, and of kith and kin, known as Weawbiny-Ket. He was the particular native American we wished to hold present imparlance with. For further advance, another canoe and another canoeist were essential. Tom was a *sine qua non*, therefore, and so was one of the two canoes he had.

George bawled loudly at the cabin, and brought out the whole domestic circle, including Tom himself, and hailed him to cross over. He launched a birch bark, and paddled it and himself into our presence. The interview was to the point, and the negotiation brief. We could have a canoe and we could have him. The legal tender required for the first was fifteen dollars, and the *per diem* in currency for the services was a dollar and a quarter. This was not hard on the collective exchequer, and we accepted the terms, the vessel and Tom. Finding that this moderate item, in our general expense account, left us a liberal margin within the estimate for the trip, we thought it would not be unthrifty to charter another Chippewa auxiliary.

The Badwater men of the tribe were out fencing deer for winter venison. The only one at hand was the tawny vagrant we first saw. He, probably, was too lazy or worthless to go fencing with his more enterprising fellows. Thebault interpreted our overtures to him. He, thinking he was the monopolist of all the present available paddling force of the hamlet, attempted to corner the market on us, and struck for three dollars a day. As in fact the aboriginal triumvirate already engaged would well suffice, his exorbitant terms were declined. When we pushed off, he gazed wistfully at the departing squadron, as if he felt he had badly overdone the business, and had made himself a too greedy instance of vaulting ambition overleaping itself.

Tom King navigated his late canoe, with High, Bissell, and part of the luggage embarked in it. Pratt, myself and the bulk of the outfit, with George and Thebault for polers, were in the larger canoe, which we named the Dickey. We set forth in high feather. This was my own first experience of birch bark navigation. The shapely and fragile coracle sat on the water gracefully and in feather-like lightness. Its treacherous unsteadiness and vagaries of equilibrium were speedily learned, and demanded a critical and ticklish nicety of poise or equilibration quite new to me. We had to bestow ourselves most cautiously, squatted on our blanket bundles, with our legs awkwardly twisted, and cramping and bending ourselves low, making it an effort and a study to maintain the trim. The facility of careening, the peril of a heedless movement turning the balance, or of tipping her over, made our probational experiences and trials in attitudes and positions, for a time, anything but assuring.

It was curious how fidgety we became and how often we wanted to shift positions, and had irrepressible tendency to motions we ought not to and dare not make. Of course, my immediate notion was, that the vaunted perfection of the canoe, as a pleasure boat, and the reputed charms of canoeing, were mythical and a tale to be told to the marines. To me, the disaster of a ducking seemed too imminent to admit of any foolishness or indiscretion. Still, High, who knew the eccentricities of the birches, had told us we would get used to all that sort of thing.

Our Menominees knew their business.. One fore and one aft, they poled the canoe along shore, with tireless steadiness, and made it speed, mile after mile, with an ease and uniformity quite admirable and surprising to us. The Tom King—as we christened our purchase from him—followed closely in our wake. High and Bissell puffingly devoted their Chicago muscle to occasional short paddling, adding their by-play of momentum to Tom's pushing. Tom surprised a wild duck napping among the grasses fringing the shore, and dispatched him with a stroke of his pole. This took the job off Pratt's hands of firing into the unwary water-fowl. By noon we had reached the mouth of the Michigami river, a few yards up which are the falls, a cascade of about thirty feet in hight, over which the whole stream rushes in one volume—but without any picturesque accessories. We ran in for lunch and to prepare for a portage.

By overland, the distance is three miles to Brulé Falls, while by river it is seven miles. We purposed sending all the load by the Dickey, and to trail to the Paint, and as that river comes in near the falls, and would have to be crossed, to portage the smaller canoe for ferriage there. We were eager to reach the river of trout sooner than we could by the water ascent, and besides, we wanted to relieve ourselves from the weariness of our compressed, and in-the-stocks-like, sitting in the canoe. The boys—for that was the term of designation of the guides among ourselves—having engaged in culinary procedure, High and I mounted our rods to employ the vacant interim in prospecting the waters for possible trout. Pratt and Bissell lazily reclined in the shade, sniffing the savoriness of the coming dinner.

We brought up close under the falls, in the moisture of the spray, for the piscatory trial. I had the mishap of slipping a foothold from a wet boulder and pitched half over and in among sharp rocks, with the slight damage of peeling a shin. High posted himself on a projecting rock and patiently whipped the foaming element with his fly for a conjectural trout, but it was love's labor lost, and when his assiduity was at length rewarded with the capture of a worthless chub, he retired with intense disgust from his coigne of rock and from the experimental sport.

But the ignominious chub proved a prelude of good luck to me. I impaled it on my hook, and threw in a shallow pool, which was foamy and froth-bubbled and an eddy below the cascade. Some unknown straggler of the fins pounced on the bait, and dashed off with a few yards of line, but flopped off without making way with the chub. It was cast again, and had barely sunk under the foam, when quick, like an electrical effect, I felt the jerk and heavy pull of some fish that would put an angler's skill to the test. It nearly pulled me off my feet. The tip of the rod snapped, and the line went buzzing down stream. The broken tip prevented playing, but I perceived the fish was struck, and began reeling up, and then found I was dragging the captive on the bottom. He made a jump which foamed the water and revealed his size, but he was fast on the hook. I slowly worked him in. When it was apparent what a monster he was, High snatched up a slab and volunteered to brain him with the timber. I declined the barbarous suggestion, and brought him ashore legitimately.

"Cast on the bank, he dies with gasping pains,
And trickling blood his silver mail distains."

It proved to be a ten pound pickerel. That catch, when taken in, made a sensation in the camp. When I mentioned High's generous offer of smashing the fish, it was noted as one of the wonders of the country to kill ducks with a pole and catch fish with a club.

. Thebault and George loaded all the outfit in the larger canoe and started it up the river. Tom shouldered the smaller one and balanced it on his head for the carry, and with it, trudged through the woods on a crooked path, as easily overcoming the obstacles of the way as any of us who only carried rods and baskets, and keeping equal pace with the party. This facility of portage, as, also, another use to which it was put, when Tom slanted it, inverted, against a tree, to shelter us all from a sudden drenching shower, went far to dispel my skepticism as to the many boasted merits of the birch bark canoe. Bissell was ambitious to catch the first glimpse of the stream which was the longed-for scene of our sport, and with this aspiration as an accelerating impulse, kept the extreme front of the line of march. When, at length, he vociferously shouted "Brulé! Brulé!" we huzzaed him back an uproarious answer, "the Brulé! the Brulé!"

The Paint coming in there was frothy and foaming with rapids. We had to run the apparently portentous ordeal to reach the further shore of the Brulé. It would be my first personal experience of the kind, and when I saw the water bursting madly over the rocks, and knew that the slightest miscalculation, or swerve, or accident, might capsize the birch or dash it in pieces on a boulder, I was, at least, a trifle anxious. But I also knew that Tom King would hold it firmly and well in hand. We were scarcely seated, when almost before one could realize it, we were swept safely through and over, and touched our feet on the bank of the Brulé.

The fishermen were ready for a trial of the rod at the very first. Eagerness became enthusiasm, and the party, excepting myself, at once sought places in which to throw their flies. I was not myself, just then, so piscatorially frantic as that "with wings as swift as meditation or the thoughts of love," I should sweep to my trouting. I preferred a leisurely stroll, to take in the situation. Straying only a few paces among the trees, I came upon a full-spread tent in which, through clouds of tobacco smoke, I discerned a party in shirt-sleeves, vigorously flipping cards in a game of old sledge. The gentleman, who said he had played the deuce for low, was first to see me, and his and my surprise were simultaneous and mutual. The surprise was for a few instants only. There was a greeting all around. I was invited to a camp-stool, and sat. Who they were and from whence, who I was, my wherefrom and whereto, were mysteries only of the brief interval in which hasty self-introductions could be exchanged. Enough of their story and of their recent travel and happenings were made known to me to enable me soon afterwards, as mutual friend, to introduce them and our party.

My comrades had straggled in, looking blank, as, in all their switching, neither had had a rise. But they forgot their chagrin in the pleasure of the new acquaintance, which was not long in being put on most friendly footing. Our tents were pitched near theirs. We were neighbors at once. But the new friends did not divert Bissell from his restless and hopeful ambition to swoop out a mess, and with his rod he started out in quest of amusement. When he rejoined us, he cackled rather triumphantly over a single puny trout he had captured, because it was the first trophy of the campaign. Our neighbors had a portable oven, and prepared us a pan of biscuit which were as light as the bulbs of foam on the water, and with them and the spread from our own supplies, we thought the refection was elegant. Had Dickey been there to observe the gusto of enjoyment by us, he would have seen that appetite had lost nothing of its healthiness by our further travel in pursuit of one.

The evening and night wore delightfully away, in a circle of both parties around the camp-fire, in gossip of sport, travel and experience by field and flood. Our neighbors had been encamped here for a week. They had trouted no further than six or seven miles up the Brulé. Their success had not been brilliant, and was not encouraging to us. But then the stream was lower than now, when it was swollen from the rains They had but just touched the region of prosperous fishing. But they soothed and consoled themselves in the confidence of making up for lost time and dearth of trout, by reprisals and compensation on the deer down on the Menominee. They were excellently equipped for that sport as well as comfortable sojourn in the woods. These gentlemen were G. D. Hayden and G. Barry of Alton, and W. W. Brown of Jacksonville. Our sociabilities with them were prolonged till late. When we retired to the blankets we were lulled into deepest sleep and into dreams by the murmur of the waters that tumbled at our feet.

# CHAPTER III.

GOOD-BYE TO NEW-MADE FRIENDS—ADVANCE ON THE BRULE—SKIRMISHING FOR TROUT—A FIRST TROUT AND WHOOP LA!—WADING FOR FISH—CAMP THEBAULT—TROUT SUPPER—METAPHYSICS—A LEAKY TENT—TABLEWARE—HIGH'S DIARIAL EFFORT—LITERARY RESOURCES—SUNDAY IN CAMP AND ON RIVER—TROUT RODS—SUNSHINE—CAMP-FIRE.

WHILE woodsmen, the weather prospects were our first concern. Beyond the range of Old Probabilities and his reports, we could only forecast the changes from the air and skies. To be drenched in the rain, or to shiver in a raw atmosphere, was not favorable to enterprises of pith and moment. The early morning signs, when we looked out and read the heavens, were portentous of showers, and boded no pleasant starting of our Alton friends downward, or of our own starting upward. The tokens, however, somewhat later, were more hopeful. The cloudiness while we were breakfasting and then smoking, partially dispersed, and fitful glimpses of sun came through, and much enlivened the prospects of the day and ourselves. The Alton party, when it was seen that no more than showers, and not torrents of rain were probable, struck its tent and shipped its *impedimenta* into the batteau; and after an exchange of warm parting civilities, embarked and rapidly dropped down out of view.

Our care was, then, to pack up and pack off. Our mission of sport would be not really begun until we were on the bosom of the Brulé. We thought ourselves weather-wise enough to predict a dry, if not clear day, so we set out hopefully. There were rapids at the mouth of the river. The Indians forced the canoes up the foaming torrent. We passed them by a flank movement on foot. High and Bissell sometimes tarried at points, and risked a footing on unsteady logs on the shore to throw a fly. The only success they had for their pains, was to permanently hang some of their tackle on obstructive limbs.

When re-embarked, Pratt and myself, with Kaquotash and Thebault, manned the large birch, and as the armament was borne by it, it was the gunboat of the flotilla. As we were now making headway into the supposed domain of deer, bear, wolf, fox, mink, muskrat and duck, it was fit that our craft should lead the advance. It was Pratt's mission to deal with any hapless creature of the Brulé animal kingdom that might appear.

Up to noon not a trout was taken. This did not dishearten us, for we had not yet touched the verge of the trout fishing proper. But, after lunch, and an hour further on, the luring fly began to strike the responsive fish. The canoes were held at a stand, by the setting poles, at intervals, and the water was vigorously whipped with casts. As a troutsman, I was the decided novice of the party. My throwing was rather wild, and Pratt was more particular about it than I was, watching it more than he did his own, and, though I did not cause him an optical catastrophe by whirling the hook in his eyes, he feared I would. As to twisting my line with his, or wrapping it round his rod, he didn't mind that much. It was merely our good luck that the canoe did not capsize, when he ducked his head down, on one side, to give my line clear swing, and threw her out of trim. His patience was above all praise. "Look out, King!" was the sharpest of his cautionary expostulations. I tried to look out, and I know he did himself, vigilantly look out. Nor had I the trained cunning of hand to securely fasten a fish. My jerking was too soon or too tardy. Pratt, however, was good enough to encourage me by telling me I would soon get my hand in.

George ran the canoe to a large boulder which parted the river into swirls below it. I preferred it for a base to cast from, rather than from the canoe, in which I did not yet dare perpendicularity. I stepped out on the rock, and cast a fresh fly. In a twinkling it was snatched at, and to my surprise, I had really struck a trout of dimensions, as was plain from the lively struggle it made. But I brought him in. It was about a fourteen-ouncer. It was the first trout I ever caught. The achievement brought down the house, and the whole party huzzaed with a will. I was once told that the sensation of catching one's first trout was akin to a father's elation over his first baby. That was a criterion of the ecstatic of which I had had only hearsay experience, but, though in the taking of the trout there was a bit of satisfaction, it did not electrify me into thrills of delight, even though my victim, by its size, dwarfed the pettier catches of the day.

The clouds began ominous lowering, and provident forethought moved us on to the intended camping place. George and Thebault knew the river and the eligibilities of shores, ground, situation, distance, etc., for encampment, and had an aforethought spot selected. In the previous summer Thebault had camped and cooked there in the service of our bar brethren, George C. Campbell and Burton C. Cook, of Chicago. We pushed on steadily, so as to forerun the rain. Bissell's taste of the sport was not satisfied with random casts from the canoe. He turned up his breeches and stepped out to wade the riffles and currents at will, in quest of more trout. He was left groping and stumbling all about in the water, to be returned for with a canoe to carry him to camp.

The camping ground was a high, steep grassy bank, at a bend, and with a space, under immense trees, already cleared for prior camps. We had come to it in complacent mood. We had made a fair start in trouting. The record of the day, not so much for its count—fifty-five—but as a promise of better yet to come, a catching that was but a cheering prologue to the more lavish performance that was to follow, was eminently satisfactory. We were just enough fagged to make rest enjoyable, and hungry enough to make the evening culinary process most appetizing. Of course our board— literally so, a box cover—was luxuriously spread with a fry of trout, the first banquet of the fins to which we sat, and that, too, with stomach enough, Indian appetites included, to clear the platters.

While George was going down to bring Bissell in from his angling waddle in the stream, he started a deer. When he afterwards told us this, Pratt pricked up his ears, taking it for granted that the buck was a straggler or forerunner of a herd not far off in the woods, and his eyes glistened at the thought that if there was such game afoot, there must be sport ahead. The mosquitoes burdened the air with their songs, but the oil and tar with which we copiously anointed ourselves served to repel them to respectful distance, until, at least, the malodorous unguent lost its effect, and then the slicking was repeated. On the whole, in that, our first camping on the Brulé, an eminent sense of satisfaction as to the day itself, and as to the prospects ahead, pervaded the whole party.

I turned in early, with a slight headache. My comrades had no idea of prematurely retiring with too much trout to healthily go to bed with; and while the camp-fire was wasting to embers and ashes, they reclined in the tent, in the fading reflection of the dying light. They were not, then, the contemplative men anglers are said to be. Between the snatches of sleep, I heard high discourse among them about Darwin, evolution, Swedenborgianism, and also other rambling profundities of theory and speculation. When their jaws wearied at last of their verbosity and of what, in my somnolence, appeared incoherent and windy twaddle, another perturbing element to prevent an "exposition of sleep" coming upon me, was a rain which set in. This of itself should have proved only a gentle lullaby to slumber, but, to the common dismay, it was found that the tent was leaky, and the shower was dripping through it.

Our concern was more for the provisions than for ourselves, and though the ponchos at hand had not been a success on the wagon route, in the way of shedding continuous torrents, they were impervious to the drip of the leaks, and the stores already in the tent were covered with rubber coats. These protected the commissariat well enough, but left us exposed to the drizzle. However, the general humidity and discomfort of the situation, and the dampness of "the drapery of the couch," did not prevent the party from finally settling into stillness again, and from slumbers that would have been refreshing if they had been more prolonged. But the mosquitoes swarmed early to their morning onset, and brought us to the scratch and fretted us mercilessly. Even the customary dope lost some of its repelling virtue. The consequence was, we were irritated and unwilling early risers.

For the breakfast, Thebault eclipsed all his previous culinary successes, in the way of fried corn-meal cakes, in Indian style. Probably a knack for preparing the native maize, in its simple and natural excellence, is an inherited or traditional trick of the native race, but, in this instance, Indian instinct was blended with enlightened art in forming a superb farinaceous product. Our *salle à manger* was the ground under spreading foliage. We squatted on blanket bundles, or on a log, for sitting at the board. The crockery and china service were platters, and cups of tin, span new. They were better to us than pieces of Sevres or porcelain. Though not decorated with any of the infinite designs or tracings of the ceramic art, in their glistening spotless lustre we could see our own broadened and grinning faces reflected.

High, thinking the shining morning calm was propitious for working up his diary, carefully fixed himself in the mossy root of a tree, opened his neat morocco-covered red-edged note book, began jotting down, for the spouse at home, the events—a kind of pilgrim's progress—of the trip. The arrearage of the past days of our itineracy, the book so far being innocent of a single diarial pencil trace, appeared too much for any reasonable patience and diligence at his command. Besides, to recall and set down the wretchedness of our first days on the road in the rain and in the dumps, was, in a degree, to renew and go through all those infelicities again. He preferred not to live them over, even by way of reminiscence. He said he was disgusted; that a diary was a plague anyhow; that his promise to his wife was neither willing nor considerate; that to keep it was not practicable; that his cue, now, was the rod and not the pencil. He was on the point of declaring an absolute rescission of the contract with his wife. I ventured to remonstrate with him, and rallied him on the enormity of his threatened recreancy to the obligations of loving and well regulated husbandry. He said he would further consider, and at least would pledge to us all that he would tabulate in his note-book the figures of our fishing.

It was Sunday, and we had the Sunday question to deal with. How to put in the day—read, sleep, fish? There was a limited supply of profane literature in camp, but not any sacred, suited to the day. No Moses or Matthew, but some Victor Hugo and Wilkie Collins. For short exercises in reading that would not over-tax the mind, I had Timb's "Century of Anecdote." All of it was pretty thin nutriment and not at all sanctifying and but slightly more entertaining. The fact was, we had an impression that reading, even novel reading, was rather out of order, or an incongruity, in a party the first postulate of whose programme was complete mental rest. The trip was intended as a furlough and off-duty to the collective and individual brains of the Chicago galaxy. By no very subtle casuistry we satisfied ourselves that literature was, therefore, not just the recreation for the day before us.

High, as the veteran, experienced in Sabbatizing in the woods, after some yawning and wearisome lounging, equipped himself for reverent diversion with the fishes, and committed himself to Tom and the canoe for combined meditation and fly-fishing, up the silent river. The example contagiously infected Pratt and myself, and, under the guidance of Thebault, our canoe was sped on the waters in similar quest of edification and trout. Bissell was truer to the day, to the traditions of his Christian ancestry, and to the teachings of the shorter catechism. He laid his rod on the slope of the tent for unbroken Sunday rest. He remained in the camp, and, on the plea of necessity, employed a considerable degree of his thoughtful reverence for the day in patching his breeches and in overhauling his rig, and then further satisfied his meditative disposition in a solemn perusal of one of Victor Hugo's romances. His sartorial efforts would have done credit to one of those nine wiseacre tailors of Tooley street.

We stopped here and there at hap-hazard to cast about us. We could get rises at nearly any point. I was more than ever satisfied how little I knew, and how much I had to learn, of trout fishing, and that I was not particularly well fitted out to learn. My earlier piscatorial experiences and trophies of any at all notable sort with game fishes were wholly those of bass-fishing in Southern Indiana. I had, without conferring with any one who could have enlightened me as to the best or the proper outfit, provided myself with only a bass rod, of perhaps eighteen ounce weight. It is true, in choosing it, I had an eye to use in the lacustral bonanzas of bass on and in reach of our route of which I had heard. But even the taste, already, of trouting had almost wholly disenamored me of bassing. The rod for bass, I now saw was not the rod for trout. Mine had too little of the whip, or of springiness, and required a more muscular arm than mine to wield it slashingly and whizzingly. Just what it was not I knew from Pratt's slender and elastic eight ounce rod, which he handled lithely and lightly, almost as freely as if it were a lady's riding whip.

We landed at the head of a small island and in the shore chute, and Pratt happened to strike a lusty trout, but in lifting it, got his rod demoralized among the limbs, and lost the fish. The river was running comparatively high, with the swell of the late rains. Most of the riffles of the normal stage were covered and swollen into smooth, swift currents. It was easily canoed with the pushing poles. They would strike bottom anywhere except in rare deep holes. The water was little roiled even with the washes of the rain; its bed was gravelly or rocky. As a consequence of the tumid volume of the stream, the trout seemed dispersed from ordinary pools, and scattered broadcast through the whole river at large, so that wherever we chose to hold up, and cast from either side, we were almost sure of striking the vagrant fish.

While out in the afternoon we were wetted with the usual shower. We very little minded a sprinkle or a moderate rain. After we returned from our cruising, Pratt went gunning, a few paces in the woods, and broke the solemn forest silence with a shot which brought down a solitary pigeon that was stupid enough to moan its loneliness in a pine-tree top so near the camp. After the evening repast we loitered around the fire, some of us diligently burning tobacco in the pipes and listening to the Indians, who related to us their forest adventures, and incidents of their trapping mink, otter, martin and beaver, in these and other regions. If we had needed more than the oppressive stillness, the deep shadows and heavy foliage which overspread us, to remind us that we were in the wilds of nature, the howl of a wolf which we heard in the distance would have been assurance enough.

## CHAPTER IV.

THE WINDFALL—RAIN AND TROUTING—BAIT-FISHING—AN EXPOSTULATORY FLY-FISHER — UNDER THE CEDARS — A NIGHT SCENE OF THE PICTURESQUE—LORENZO PRATT'S FRIVOLITY—ADIEU TO WINDFALL—THE FUTURE CAMP—A LANTERN HUNT ORGANIZED—BISSELL AS A MEDICINE-MAN.

Though we had slept coldly and brokenly, it was joyous in the morning to greet, with opening eyes, a full flush of sunshine and a cloudless sky, really the first of the trip. These happy auspices were enjoyed and hailed by us as signs of weather fairness and bettering, and of splendor for the day, at least, and we hoped for many days. Before leaving, the camp was formally christened Camp Thebault, in honor of him whose masterly cunning in the kitchen department had won the good opinion of us all.

With exhilaration and bright as the glow of the morning, we embarked for up-river, and for a time on the way, the beams of the sun touched the rip-

ples, made by our cutting the water, into dazzling sparkles. But after all and after a while, the cheering resplendence proved delusive and fleeting. The day, ere long, turned out to be like one of April,
> "Which now shows all the beauty of the sun,
> And by and by a cloud takes all away."

As it were, a dim smoke, a shadow, crept up in the west, and soon formed into a cloud which rapidly advanced and spread. If not portending a storm, it, at least, boded a shower. The full capacity of propelling power was applied to hurry us to the Windfall. This is a point fifteen miles from the mouth of the river, where a tornado had leveled the forest at some not remote period. We could, at the same time, dine and shelter there.

To make for and reach the Windfall before the rain was then all that our foresight and timely pressing speed barely enabled us to do. The Menominees got the tent set almost in a jiffy, and we and the cargo were no more than under cover, when a most copious rain began. On the way up, we had not been idle or indifferent as to trouting, but had vigorously slashed the lines on the water, tarrying briefly by a tree, a log, under riffles, or alongside of a boulder, or in a smooth reach. The baskets were plentifully replenished, and with choicer spoils, on the average, than those of previous sport. There had been other Brulé voyagers here at some former season. We discovered, in the bushes, an abandoned birch-bark, in a stage of decrepitude which showed that its career of floating was ended. A sorry looking rusted camp kettle, also, hung on a branch near by it. Like ourselves, doubtless the navigators of the craft had put in at so forbidding a point, under a stress of necessity. There was not a single attractive feature in the whole landscape.

We appeased the customary noon-day hunger on a trout dinner. The rain had abated sufficiently to allow of frying by the camp fire. In a pause of the elements, High sallied out with his rod, and, from a neighboring log, essayed the stream a short while, and was successful in killing a number of handsome fish. He quoted an accepted piscatory authority that trout will not rise after a rain, and now claimed that his replete basket avouched a different story as to the ready hungering propensity of Brulé trout, at least. Seeing the results of this breeze of prosperity that set upon High even under the cloud, all of us ventured on an afternoon trouting cruise. High and I had our canoe guided up stream. I brought to the boat one of the mammoths of the water. George reached out to seize it, but it flopped off, and shot away like a lightning flash.

We had wandered some distance from camp, when the remorseless clouds suddenly trooped up again, from all quarters. The densest shower of the day burst upon us. We as well as our comrades in the other birch, made for a group of towering cedars over-branching the water, and laid by underneath. We harbored there an hour, patiently waiting the stop or slackening of the down-pour, all the while, too, the percolating drops pelting us until we were "demnition moist." There was no surcease, and but little moderating of the rain, and after all our pains to escape a shower-bath, we were forced to face the watery music and run the effusive gauntlet down to camp. Spite of the day's adverse conditions, though, we could compute sensations of pleasure to an aggregate of one hundred and forty-five, for the party, those being the figures of joint capture.

While out with High, I tried a pink fragment of Pratt's pigeon on my hook. It proved a taking dainty for the trout, and with it, I snapped them up vigorously, for me, at least. This sort of fishing was an abomination, and utterly immitigable, to High. It was bait-fishing, and baiting for trout, whether the bait were worm, flesh, fowl, fish or natural insect, or whatever else, was simply a gross and vulgar folly. Fly-fishing is the only fishing for him. He was our artistic and expert trout angler. He had victoriously trouted in the Rocky Mountain regions, and has proud memories of Bear and Snake river salmon-trout. He is a learned pundit and *savan* in the genesis and products of artificial-fly entomology. His own fly-book is a curiosity shop of the vagaries and inventions of insect manufacture, a petty museum of gim-cracks made of wire, hair, floss, feathers and tinsel, called flies, probably because they have so little resemblance to any known creatures of the natural fly family. These are to him the only allowable trout lures and deceits.

Bait, therefore, to High is a scarcely pardonable impiety, and nothing less than piscatory barbarism. The fellow that trouts with fish, flesh or fowl, he thinks, will never come to any good, and justifies Doctor Johnson's crabbed fleer, that angling is a stick and a string with a worm (or bait) at one end, and a fool at the other. But for all his reprobatory pantomime of features, I kept myself on the best of terms with the trout, and persisted in enticing them with slices of pigeon. He, also, practices constant casting, with the rod-arm in perpetual see-sawing, to barely tip the water with the fly, and then give it a back over-shoulder throw for a cast again from behind; or sometimes he tickles the stream with his tackle, by skipping it along the surface. In the flogging mode of casting, I could not pretend to be his peer. A thought of rivaling him in it would have been absurd, if only for the reason that my flexors and extensors were constitutionally unequal to such practice with eighteen ounce tackle.

When the starless, beclouded night came on, our group, the tents and canoes, presented a striking scene of the picturesque. Our pyre of pine trunks was blazing near our tent; the other, the cooking fire, being further in front. The canoes were on the ground, turned up on edge and at right angles with each other, forming a half square aflank the native's burning log heap, to make a shelter for their sleeping. The firelight flickering in their dusky visages as they moved and stole about in luminous relief against the night beyond, with their ceaseless chatter of Menominee, seeming to alienize them still more to our fancies, or to sound as mysterious voices of the night, gave them a weird or phantom-like aspect, or made them seem apparitions, like the Macbeth witches—" on the earth but not of it."

We had hardly ceased musing on the scene of the nocturnal picturesque, when Pratt surprised us by an ill-timed pleasantry. The untoward news had come to us from the chief of the scullery, that the caddy of lard was nearly exhausted. This commodity was so important an element in the cookery of the camp, that a total deficit thereof was regarded as a dispensation too serious for serene contemplation. As a matter touching the food question, it was a vital point, and we thought it was trifling with the gravity of the prospect for Pratt to inflict upon us a bit of heartless jocularity by telling us that it had been a doubt with High and Bissell, whether a caddy of lard should be added to our stores, as a needful supply; but, for his part, he thought it "safest to be on the *lard's* side," and had, therefore, brought the useful caddy along. This grim and irreverent facetiousness only provoked from us the withering rebuke of silence which promptly subdued him. We hid ourselves in the blankets to sleep. It may have been a deserved retribution that Pratt's wicked joke, possibly, had perturbed him in the night, like a horrid phantom returning to plague the inventor, for, in the morning he complained of unwonted insomnia.

We were prompt enough to make a start from the Windfall. We had only run in there for protection against the rain. It was a low, flat ground, thickly luxuriant with bushes and alders. The few trees left by the tornado stood out, apart, and skeleton-like, gaunt and branchless, the naked trunks blasted and charred by fire, which, at some time, blew in gusts of flame over what the breath of the tempest spared. None of us slept comfortably. The air was damp, raw and chilly, and sleeping in couples, the joint exertions of both the pairs were unequal to the problem of warmth and comfort. Thus far, this was the only occasion of coolness between any of us. High was an experienced Rocky Mountain blanketeer, and knew more than any of us about sleeping out of nights, and, also, from his army teaching, had learned what manner of blanket would be needed. His red and gray California blankets were of a size and weight to make ours, in the comparison, seem mere airy, thin apparitions of blankets. Bissell, as his bed-fellow, got their benefit.

These were not arctic latitudes by any means, but here, even in August, which down at Chicago usually burns with something of tropical heat, thick clothing, stuffs of wool, instead of flax or cotton, are necessities of open-air life. The coat one wears against the blast of a norther from Lake Michigan, and the heavy undershirt one takes to his bosom, when the Fahrenheit marks zero, and the cutting January air whistles along the South Park boulevard, are the garments for all nights, and for frequent days, on a summer voyage on the Brulé. The hemlocks are always spoliated for boughs, for a ground stratum on which to spread the blankets. Their elasticity and balsamic breath seem to be a happy contrivance of nature for the very purpose of supplying such satisfying use.

The further limit of our bearings and departures was a point about fifteen or sixteen miles up from the mouth. It was the intention to pitch the tent there for the longest sojourn. From that point, is a trail to a triplet of small lakes, separated by short distances. The water-sheets are called Boot Lakes. The first of them is noted as fertile in bass and as a resort for deer. We looked forward to the vicinage of the lakes of Boot as our land of promise for venison. The Indians spoke hope's flattering tale to us of the plenty of deer that frequented the region. Our autochthones hunt them at night, and in the canoe, with a dark lantern. While the birch is creeping along shore, they are concealed behind a bark shield, with the light in front of it streaming out ahead. The animals in the bushes, or splashing in the water, when cropping the grasses or water-lilies, on the brink or in the sloughs, are dazed and bewildered by the glare, and stand still as if spell-bound, while their eyes glare luminously from the reflection, making them a shining mark for the hunter, who is stealing closely on them, so that the shooting is easy and the result nearly certain.

Boot lake trail was reached in the afternoon. In the usual tarrying by the way, we had intervals of sport in which the waters were flagellated so prosperously that we punished more of the trout than we could use, returning the useless ones to the water. The appearance of the camping ground was far from captivating. A little island fronted it across a petty groove of stream. It was a flat situation, and adjacently it was marshy. A small spring oozed out near at hand, and a tiny limpid rill of coldness flowed—enough to supply our drinking cups with pure draughts. There was just enough dry, sandy surface for camp use. There was only the shade of a ragged tree over the tent. But as our business was fishing, we would be but little at the camp, and when there, for the most part the night would hide its uninviting aspects in the common obscurity.

We began to sate, or rather the appetite lost much of its keenness in the superfluity of trout, and our desire was now for venison. We were on the tip-toe of expectation for diet of deer. Our first concern, when our house was set in order, was to prepare for a hunt that very night. Tom King and Thebault were to try their hands as deer-slayers, and at six o'clock they filed out on the path to Boot lake, with a shouldered canoe, which, however the hunting might turn out, was to be left at the lake for bassing next day, specially for my benefit. Bissell had been seized by the preposterous whim of taking a little exercise, and was not to be laughed out of it, and went along merely to ply his legs. On his return in a couple of hours, he gave us to understand that he had had all the gratuitous exercise he wanted—quite enough for all the trip—and was a tired but a wiser man.

We were doubtful about the prospering of the deer enterprise. As it cost us nothing, and the Indians were to bear the burden of the work, while we only bore the burden of suspense, we had encouraged them to the attempt, in the face of unfavorable conditions. One of these was the moon, which shone through the clouds. The other was the windiness. These turned the chances against success. The deer scent keenly when a breeze is stirring. The illumination pales in the moonlight. Our men, for want of a lantern, provided a screen of bark with a candle in a split. It was liable to flare or blow out in the wind. Though by no means sanguine, we hoped for success. Our imaginations pictured deer, and all the mouths in camp watered for venison. I had a headache that throbbed and throbbed me. Bissell put his versatile wits at work to devise me some relief, assuming to act as medicine-man and therapeutist. I preferred the headache to his prescribed remedies. Finally, he prescribed Doctor Sangrado's invariable panacea—warm water, without the blood-letting. I swallowed about a quart of the Brulé, tepid and salted. The pickle really helped to relieve me in the manner predicted.

## CHAPTER V.

TOO MOONSHINY—MINK MARAUDERS—GOING A-BASSING—
BOOT LAKE—ROUGH TRAIL—BROILED BASS FOOD FOR MINKS
—THE WHOLE HOG GONE—LAST DAY AT UPPER CAMP—DOE
AND FAWNS—RED SQUIRRELS—LIVELY TROUTING—RETRO-
GRESSIVE AND DOWNWARD—CAMP OCCUPATION—MOSQUI-
TOES.

THE candle-bearers returned at midnight. They brought in nothing but themselves, and were so tired they could hardly do that. Tom King told the whole story of failure sententiously when he said, "It too much moonshine," at the same time glancing spitefully at the moon. They had seen a couple of deer, but in truth the deer had seen them, too, and their velocity of departure was something marvelous. But Tom said we would have enough of deer in going down the Menominee, and on the strength of that soothing prediction, we resumed our slumbers. While we slept, the enemy came and despoiled us of the breakfast mess. The pick of the day's trout had been dressed, and laid out over night in beautiful array, on the provision box, right close to the nostrils of George, where he must have been frightfully snoring, as was his wont, under the canoe. The minks stole a march on the sleeping sentinel at his post, and made a foray on the fish, and portaged the entire lot to their holes. This mishap was the occasion of various impromptu expressions of temper in emphatic vernacular phrases, as well as in voluble Indian lingo.

As well in respect of other supplies, as in the case of the lard, we had miscalculated the relations of demand and supply. Our appetitive faculties increased from the start, so much at odds or out of tally with the appetitive supply, that we were fairly running short of stores. To meet the contingency we should have to moderate the consumption, reduce the rations, or change our base, and that, too, speedily. There was already a potato dearth in the camp, and by some of the party the esculent tubers were thought as much a staff of life as bread itself. In this fact of scarcity alone, we foresaw an early retrogressive move.

The weather omens were, at first, unpropitious for the intended bassing at Boot lake. The sky was sullen with clouds that threateningly hovered, and in the earlier hours we were dismal indeed, with a prospect of a stupid, lagging day on the camp ground; but we knew the fickleness of the elements here; and, surely enough, just like themselves, ere a great while the "base, contagious clouds" vanished, leaving not a rack behind. The Boot lake business then came on the tapis. I was the only volunteer ready to respond. Bissell had disenchanted himself of any more Boot lake, by his supererogatory and romantic exercise over there the last evening, and to go again was like the task of Sisyphus. Pratt and High had no fancy for bass, and still less for the miserable trail that led to them. Still, they admitted it was reasonable that I should have a fair field for bassing, and that the expedition should proceed. A canoe was already awaiting it on that placid water. Who was to be my companion there was settled only by an impartial conscription by lot. Bissell drew the short twig from High's disinterested fingers, and was elected. Pratt and High slyly tipped themselves the wink, and happily twirled the longer twigs, the tokens of their better luck, and quietly chuckled at their escape from trials of the route and from the tamer sporting for bass when so much superb trouting was more handy.

The pathway to the lake was nearly a mile of all the worst features of a forest trail. We had logs to climb over or leap, bogs and swamps to flounder in, hills to scuffle up, ravines to cross, briars to scratch us, and bushes to switch in our faces. How a canoe could be made to furrow its way through those woods was a mystery, but it had been done. We struck the leg part of the boot-shaped lake at a beaver dam, launching there, and had to paddle through a little wilderness of reeds, water-lilies, sunken branches and scattered logs, so intertangled that passage was a matter of patience and trouble. Both Thebault and Tom grunted with the task. But once in full swing on the clear, deep water of the foot-shape of the lake, we were ready for business in the noted haunt of bass. It is according to Gunter to bass with minnows for bait. But it was impossible to capture a single one, and we were compelled to fall back on pork.

It was short experience to find that the adipose tissue of the unclean flesh was as killing a bait as the minim of fins. My pinch of bacon fat had but just left a greasy film and sunk under the surface, when it was snapped up and run away with, several fathoms length of line. I was equal to the occasion, and hauled in a thumping green bass. Bissell's bait of pork was appropriated with like prompt voracity, and he hitched on his trout-rod a three-pounder of shining viridescence, which sorely tested the elasticity and strength of his wand. And so it went on. The fish so eagerly took the hook, and the playing in was such heavy, dull and simply muscular business, that it was more work than play to catch them. My line presently took a freak of twisting and fouling, and so the reel clogged and worked badly, or not at all; but, in truth, the fun was too tame and unexciting to warrant the repeated requirement of time and patience to set the tackle to rights, and I early and willingly rested from my labors. Bissell, too, soon tired of a monotony that he fancied was not much sport and was a good deal of toil. We had parted eleven of the bass from their native element. Besides, a breeze had sprung up and roughed the waters into wavelets. We were quite willing to give it our adieus and leave Boot lake to its usual solitude. The canoe, the bass and ourselves were in camp again at noon.

The sky was now clear, and more of the infinite azure was seen than on any of our days. We availed ourselves of such an auspicious circumstance to give apparel and blankets an airing. They were hung around to take the genial sunshine and the ventilating breeze, but scarcely added any picturesqueness to the scene. While Tom and Thebault were clinking the kettle and pan, and preparing the bass to be served for dinner, Bissell and I shaded ourselves in the tent and scribbled; he was sketching our trip for the press, and read to me some of his graphic touches. High and Pratt had been doing a forenoon cruise, but as they never were known to lag superfluous anywhere or far-off when dinner smelt ready to their educated and hankering nostrils, they were in on time. They brought a fine mess of trout, which were speedily consigned to the frying pan, and then served on the board, and our appetite being edged up to nicety and delicacy on them, the grosser course—fry of bass—was distasteful, and after a few morsels eaten, was ignominiously dispensed with, and the whole lot of Boot lake spoil was chucked into the bushes, as rubbish for the minks.

Bissell and I started the canoe out in the afternoon to skim some of the neighboring waters. The angling was all well enough until my rod got in the way of disjointing itself in the cast, the last joint and the tip, with the line running from the reel, and dropping in the water. Two or three instances of this severance of the pieces were tolerable, but when it became habitual, the mishap was calculated to make one a trifle irritable. The means were not at hand to remedy the mischief, and as this was a nuisance to Bissell as well as vexation to me, in a degree spoiling his sport and entirely ruinous to mine, I had myself pushed back to camp. He, with one of the boys, started out again in further pursuit of his mission, and it proved to be a prosperous one.

High and Pratt had also enriched themselves with much booty of the Brulé. The day's total return was one hundred and seventy-three. We learned at the camp fire that the subsistence department was almost depleted of pork and potatoes. They were prime articles of consumption. As a staple in the woods, no fish, other flesh, or fowl, can compare with the products of the indispensable hog. A pound of a porker up on the Brulé is worth more, for steady diet, than some scores of trout. We needing the essential pig, the question of longer staying virtually settled itself. To retrace our course was, therefore, a necessity, but a much regretted one. Here our sport had been, and would continue, best and most generous.

The last night at this camp was peculiar for its splendid moonlight and its sharp air. All the covering at command was put to service for our sleeping. The breakfast trout had been precautionally placed in the tent under common guard, to secure them from the furtive minks, and furnished us a choice repast early, while yet the roseate hues of morning tinged the east. We purposed making a last full half day's ranging of the waters, and so to make the most of the time. High and myself, with Kaquotash as our canoeist, stemmed the current upwardly.

While rounding a bend, an exciting view presented itself. On the point of an island, directly facing us, and a fair mark, in gun range, stood a doe and twin fawns. The sun on the water must have dazzled them, for they were motionless, a couple of minutes. This was my first sight of deer on the trip; in fact, it was the first of my life, of wild deer in the woods. I thought I now knew something of the buck-fever I had heard of, and was realizing some of those *sui generis* febrile symptoms in the excitement and thrill of the scene. The sight was a kind of fascination. We held ourselves motionless, too, from fear of breaking the spell. We could only gaze, wonder and admire. Pratt's gun and projectiles, of course, were lying in their cover, in harmless disservice in the away-off camp. We could only enjoy the view as a matchless picture of grace and beauty. All at once the doe pricked up her ears, seeing or scenting danger, and whirled around her white tail on us, the fawns doing the same, and all stampeded into the bushes. The tableau vanished like an instantly dissolving view.

We scared a saw-bill duck into fits, from a nook of water, under a clump of bushes, where we surprised it napping, and heard its obstreperous squawk and flapping of the water far in the distance. We frequently heard pigeons humming their wings. At the camp, or near about, was a community of small red squirrels. One of these ruddy free foresters seemed to haunt, or be partial to a particular tree which he thought was a convenient observatory of our camp. He liked to cock upon a limb, wagging his brush, and keeping his quizzing eyes in our direction. He and myself came to know each other by sight, and allowed ourselves the privilege of mutual close approach and free parley. Once, when he presumed too much on his short acquaintance, and impudently chattered at me, I flung a chunk at him just to teach him manners. The projectile was a lesson not exactly to his taste, and he was not afterward so friendly, and quit frisking among the branches of our trysting tree. How much game there might be in the depths of the woods, and what it is, were not known to us, much less was it sought by us. Stalking the forest to hunt would be a task of such difficulty in the face of almost impassability, that, even with the stoutest legs, the most dauntless spirit would recoil from it.

The trouting that morning was exceptionally superb. Our Menominee appeared to have an instinct when and where to halt. Generally the fish jumped as fast as we could throw, and, like little meteors, they shot and shot again. Sometimes, as if in a freak of playfulness, the same fish dashed in and out in hop, skip and jump style. In one cast made, the same trout, by actual count, leaped a dozen times after the fly, which was tweaked or skipped along the surface without re-throwing. This one was a nimble tumbler, and flirted pretty somersaults in chase of the tantalizing fly in the neatest way.

To me, a novice, much of the charm of fly-fishing was in the brilliant, sometimes comical, leaping activities and topsy-turvy inversions of the trout. They vaulted in all the forms of grace and beauty, and looked like flashing jets or spurts of color from the stream. They frisked as readily at the touch of my fly to the water as they did at the knack with which High allured them. But he had the cunning of the experienced angler in his hand—that timely skillful twitching of the wrist which gives the killing touch which marks much of the difference between the angling verdant and the veteran. It was that deft knack of wrist that made any trifling or nonsense about his hook dangerous to the trout, and, in the count, made him come out with great numbers ahead of me.

On return to camp, the traps were found ready and arranged for departure, and it was but brief manipulation to prepare the trout and serve them for the feast. It was a penury, not of trouting sport, but of staple provisions that impelled us to a returning movement. By a vigorous parsimony in pork, and similar economy in potatoes, in pinching contrast to the careless profuseness of those substantials, with which we had, all the way, marched into the bowels of the land, we had up to this very lunch, eked out some of each to serve our needs. But now, the tale was told, *fuit porcus, solanum tuberosum non est,* the whole hog was gone and the wholesome tuber is not!

After carving on a memorial tree the names of the party, and the official returns of our trouting exploits, we embarked with something of sorrow, but with naught in anger, from the cheerless locality.

The forenoon vagrancy had been so fertile of sport, and so rich in the rarest loot of the stream, in fact, we were so satisfied with trouting, that it was only a very promising or exceptionally tempting pool or place, that could prick the sides of our intent to any further piscatory trials. As many as we needed of the trout captured on the way we stored in the baskets, and the surplus was returned to the stream for piscicultural purposes at any rate. We passed the Windfall with much felicitation, that there was no stress or predicament forcing us to harbor there again. We had the calm and glory of a golden sunset attending us when we rounded in, and struck the brink at Camp Thebault again.

As soon as we touched the shore, with ready commotion of wings, the mosquitoes swarmed to greet us with a gory and rapacious welcome. There appeared an eager rivalry in each particular sucker of our veins to be first of the swarm to imprint on our faces a bloody and pitiless salute. The benign extract of olive and pine was liberally spread over us, until like an oil of joy, it made the countenance to shine. The process was repeated.

While Thebault was exercising his official functions of the kitchen, Bissell and Pratt had a mild attack of polite literature. The first gentleman was giving himself an insight into the high life of the last century through Timb's anecdotes. It was an open question as to Pratt, who was worrying himself over a Wilkie Collins' novel, and with a host of mosquitoes, at the same time, which excited his most lively interest and attention—the plot and personages of the book, or the bloody, biting fiends whirling and buzzing on the wing. High propped himself on a huge pine root, and in an exemplary mood of dutiful regard for his promise and his wife, penciled in his diary. Of the firkin that contained our butter, possibly oleomargerine, I improvised an easy chair and made notes of the excursional history. The reading and the writing though were not satisfactory. The entire party, with prompt unanimity, was then, and at all times, most happy to swap a feast of reason for a feast of victuals. A diet of fish was the brain nutrition for which we waited.

# CHAPTER VI.

BOILED TROUT—ADIEU TO THE BRULE—THE MICHIGAMI AGAIN—SHOWER AND TORRENTS—BADWATER HAMLET AND KING'S CABIN—DEER-FENCING—OJIBBWA LITERATURE—A TROUT STREAM AND A TROUT'S IGNOBLE FATE —BADWATER LAKES—A DISTANT DEER.

WITHOUT pork or lard the fry was done for. The next best thing, as a culinary expedient for serving trout, was broiling. We were now reduced to this. We had a patent broiler, heretofore unused. That utensil was now in demand. But when intended to be utilized it was found ridiculously unequal to the needs of the occasion. Broiling on an extended scale had not been contemplated, and only for a bit of occasional roasting to suit a momentary whim of taste, the device had been provided. But it had only a capacity of three trout at one toasting. Our forest-sharpened hunger was usually too keen and devouring to wait on courses of three fish for four men of robust and full-grown appetite. But

Kaquotash luckily knew a thing or two about broiling a collective mess. He extemporized a broiler from a slender alder branch, and splitting it and placing eight or ten of the fish between the splits, bound together with thongs of bark, he thrust the branch in the ground slanting over the coals. Thus a whole batch of trout was grilled at one and the same time, and broiled and crisped to a charm. When we saw how much the contrivance of Indian wit eclipsed the Yankee patent invention, we indignantly hoisted the wire fraud and delusion into the middle of the Brulé.

By some insidious and mysterious means High had inveigled Thebault to boil a few trout and set them before us. The discovery of the boiled trout almost incited a riot in the camp. The folly of subjecting a brook trout to the hot and geyser-like bubbling, 212° Fahrenheit, to the utter washing out and annihilation of the delicate and subtle flavor, and reducing the fish to paste, and leaving it as insipid and tasteless as a boiled rag, was a culinary blunder and crime. It was an abomination that could only find its match in some of the fish dishes of the dinner served up in the manner of the ancients in "Peregrine Pickle." The peace was preserved, however, by pitching the sickish and viscous pulp into the river, though High himself was not heaved in with it.

According to the custom of all trouters and

saunterers on the Brulé, we left memorials of our trouting and presence inscribed in names, words and figures, on a barked pine tree, to tell to all to whom such presents should come greeting, our story of piscatorial exploits. Here our angling practically ended. We had nothing to do but to commit our barks to the downward way, and take it easy. We landed for the portage around the falls, near the mouth, and halted at the camping ground long enough to add there, also, on a tree, the statistics of our fishing, and to recall reminiscences of our Alton friends. The rather formidable rapids just at the camp, now that we were familiar with the canoe and with Indian skill and mastery, we had no hesitation in venturing to shoot, and enjoyed the excitement of bounding down through the tossing waters.

When our fleet was embosomed on the broader and calmer stream, the paddles sped it along smoothly and rapidly ahead of the swift current, giving to us all the luxury of delicious motion. We swept into the mouth of the Michigami and rounded to, at the point where the marvelous pickerel was brought in. A meagre lunch, the remains of our store of provisions, was served us on a bleached pine log, stranded there by some Michigami freshet. During the interval there I threw in a hook with a scrap of trout, to try for another phenomenal fish. But the call might as well have been for spirits from the vasty deep, as for bass or pickerel.

The Menominee river here really begins, and the scenery becomes striking and picturesque. The shores are partly hills and swells crowned with magnificence of foliage, in summer glory of luxuriance and green.

The next objective point was Badwater and Tom King's cabin. Before we were far afloat, our seemingly inevitable and pitiless fate, dark clouds, gathered behind and portentously loomed towards us. The boys lustily swung the paddles, and the barks sprang and leaped to the strokes, cleaving the water like things of abounding life. But the clouds, like a rushing, bannered host, massed and marched rapidly, gaining on us, and, at last, the lighter skirmish van overtaking us, we were moderately showered, and, in moistened plight, we hurried into the cover of the sheltering hospice. We were fortunate in making the refuge of Tom King's castle of pine just in time. The showering was a petty overture only to the rain-storm that followed it, and which, as if all the windows of heaven had opened widest, poured in torrents. The clatter of the rain on the bark roof was dinning, but it was not unpleasing music.

While the storm was wildly driving, two drenched and be-draggled Chippewas, living across the river, the most abject and forlorn looking of redskin ragamuffins, returned from a deer-fencing enterprise, and, with a vociferous hullabaloo signalled for a canoe to cross them over. Fencing is an Indian mode of deer hunting. A line of fallen trees and branches, making a rude *cheval de frise*, is laid and arranged from east to west, between two points, sometimes several miles apart, at intervals of which the hunters are stationed. At the season when the deer travel south and come to the fence, instead of leaping or forcing through it, they face about and pace alongside, and passing the hidden Indian on his watch, are easily shot from the cover. This kind of ambuscading supplies most of the winter venison. Such killing seems more a massacre or butchery than sport.

While we were drying our wet clothes, we took a survey of the cabin. There was a good deal of the white as well as of the red-man in the household. Most of the furniture was of the usual plain sort. In place of Axminster carpeting or drugget, there was an Indian many-colored, woven grass matting, laid on part of the floor, which was smooth, glistening neat pine. The bed-covers were a patch-work of the brightest and gaudiest colors. Parts of the walls were profusely and jumblingly pasted with Harper, Frank Leslie and other pictorial prints and cartoons, a maze of wood-cuts, the only embellishment or art pretension in the room.

Tom had a library of sacred literature—the New Testament in English, which he could not read, and the New Testament in Ojibbwa (Chippewa) which he could read, but apparently did not. The aboriginal evangel excited my curiosity. I took a shy at it, to see how the gospels ran in Chippewa vernacular, and began the investigation in comparative philology, with the first verse, first chapter, of Matthew: "*Mesu oo otian i Reb-ematiziani-Muzinaugun au Jesus Christ inu dabidum oouisum gaio inu Abrahanum.*" The twenty-four lettered word, almost an alphabet, was too much for me as a totality. I tried it in sections and by installments, with no better result—it was a poser in orthoepy, and beyond my power to vocalize. Ojibbwa may be a pleasing dialect, but some of its parts of speech are rather long-drawn-out, and the syllables, in many words, run too far tandem to be conveniently rolled as sweet morsels of speech under the tongue.

Tom handsomely played host to us. He was liberal of his plain civilities. He wanted us to feel we had the freedom of the house. His tawny spouse, in speech, was nothing, if not Chippewa, and had nothing to say to us, but performed her part in the etiquette of the occasion with a pantomime of features quite as meaning of cordiality and welcome as if phrased in the formulas of the best society. She certainly won her way to our hearts and stomachs by the excellent supper set before us. The fried dried venison was a specially native dish that seemed to have a flavor and gaminess and wildness racy of the wigwam and the forest. The sauce of raspberries, picked from near-by bushes, and the syrup from the tap of maples on the hill, were so choice that by a mistake of appropriation, or thoughtlessly, we quite overstepped the etiquette which constrains guests from emptying a host's dishes, and not enough of either was left to serve as a bare hint of what it was.

As Tom King had not caught the parental usage of many civilized good families, of turning the children loose in the drawing-room to practice their hilarious infantile diversions and general boisterousness for the entertainment and admiration of guests, the juvenile fraction or fractions of the household were secluded, doubtless to temporary exile and silence in the kitchen corner. Tom and his helpmate, also, themselves occupied that small apartment for the night. They assigned to us the two beds, in what was chamber, dining and drawing-room, with their gay butterfly-like overspreads. These coverlets were light and as bright and gay as the dream of a tropical flower-garden.

Early next morning, Tom saddled a horse, and set out for a trip to Dickey's, to procure supplies for our use—possibly, too, for his own. Our pine box pantry told a beggarly tale of emptiness. He had *carte blanche* to bring us such commodities of sustenance as that limited market would afford. The whole day would be required for the accomplishment of his mission of food, and was before us for disposal.

With a trout stream only two miles distant, of which we had most favorable hearsay, High was not the man to lazily dawdle away a good clear angling day in an Indian cabin. The chance of sport there was the more alluring from the fact that a pale-face angler was said never to have cast a line or his shadow in the petty stream. High thought, doubtless, it would very notably feather his cap to be, of all civilized fly-anglers, the pioneer to the mysterious and occult water. In the glamour of his vision of the venture, Pratt, also, discerned a degree and *eclat* of novelty. Both, therefore, on the directions given by Tom, took the trail and the hazard of losing it, and themselves, too, in the woods.

Bissell and myself rather preferred enjoying convenient scenery, and, with George and the canoe, set out on an excursion to a panorama of the scenery of Badwater lakes. These sheets are a chain of irregularly shaped lakelets opening one into another—perhaps more than a half-dozen of them—said to be called Badwater from the reputed dark shade of the water. The portage to them is a half-mile, over a steep ridge, and starts from the river a mile below Tom King's place. Of course the canoe was indispensable, both to carry us on the river and to cruise us on the lakes. Fishing for bass and pickerel was to be merely an incident, not the purpose, of the excursion, an exploration of the lakes and a view of the scenery being the main intent.

As George told us there would be a chance to sight a deer, Bissell took Pratt's artillery and munitions of war for the benefit of the contingent deer. It is questionable whether the gunner had a remote idea of killing the hypothetical stag, should one be obliging enough to appear, but the ambition to try was laudable and natural. We skirted, when afloat, round about, and crossed some of the lakes, when finally George, with his telescopic eye, descried a deer a half mile away, browsing the shore herbage. After a series of observations, Bissell got his eye on it, and was seized with the usual buck fever of the novice. The deer was not disposed to await closer familiarity, after its first windward sniff of the enemy, but forthwith took to its hoofs, leaving to the excited man-at arms but the poor satisfaction of no other than a very distant and perfectly harmless shot.

Our lunching place was a beautiful, smooth, high and shaded knoll, from which there was a fine view of curving shores and rich foliage in every direction. Though not grand, the scenery was charming and lovely—a picture for a landscape artist. The fate of the daily shower followed us here, but the sun appeared soon enough to dry us into comfort. The lakes are supposed to abound in bass and pickerel. Bissell put out a trolling line, and I used the rod. My pork bait was a failure. But Bissell's spoon was attractive enough to allure three several bass to a miserable fate. George, too, let out a tarnished spoon on a length of line, and alternately paddled and fingered the trolling appliance, and had the fortune of capturing a greenish four-pound bass.

The fishing was not an exciting amusement. The perfect calm of the water, the stillness of the air, and the repose of the whole scene were so effective that we yielded to their drowse-like influence, and only gently and languidly glided in the canoe. A pair of loons, mournfully crooning, a duck, the deer, were the only living objects on or at these silent waters. On the return way to the cabin, and at some rapids near Tom's, we disembarked, left the canoe, and started to walk through the woods. Unexpectedly, a covey of partridges started up from the ground, and Bissell fired a random charge at the flock, but it was a wild shot. One of the birds perched on a near limb, and quietly watched Bissell re-loading, and apparently waited for the shot. George and I stood by in expectation of a partridge for the pot. Bissell blazed away, and made the feathers fly—away with the fowl to parts unknown.

Rounding over the hill at Tom's, we were greeted with a roaring *whoop-la* from High and Pratt, who had just returned from the trout stream. Their vociferation was meant as a triumphal shout, as we knew presently, when they told their story of

the day. Their exploits threw ours in the shade.
The four bass of our party, the deer not shot and
the partridge not bagged, were not to be glorified
in view of the fifty-one handsome trout in their
baskets, taken from the hidden nooks of the unfamed
stream. It was a brooklet winding darkly under
the shadows of tangled, interlacing forest growths,
and so obscurely creeping or wriggling its way
through the dense wood that it is not singular that
it was reported to have been ever untouched of a
white man's fly.

In this tiny water-run, so hard to be reached and
to be fished, and so unpromising of more than small
fry, but in a segment of natural meadow, in and
out of which it wound, Pratt was fortuned with the
most brilliant piscatorial *coup* of the trip; that is, a
prize trout, more than a full pounder, tinged and
speckled in the richest emblazonry of his species.
The peerless beauty was landed and unhooked, clean
out in the meadow grass, but, as gamey in our element as in its own, struggled desperately, and in its
expiring convulsion, ingloriously flopped plump
into a muskrat hole.

That a paragon trout should be converted to the
base uses of a musquash's meal was, indeed, a startling *contretemps*, and "if 'twere not to consider too
curiously to consider so," in its small way, an instance of the cruel irony of fate, of a kind with that
final ignominy of a hero dead and turned to clay

stopping a hole to keep the wind away. Indeed, there was a mixture of the ludicrous and pathetic in the ignoble fate of Pratt's splendid trout. But over the grievous mischance to the fish and to himself, he kept a manful composure, and bore himself as one that could smile at grief, and possess his soul in patience against either the jests or the calamities of outrageous fortune. It was noted by us all that, at the evening repast, his emotional nature had not so worked on his appetite as to impair his healthy capacity of getting away with his accustomed share of trout and all wholesome viands.

# CHAPTER VII.

FIRST FROST—ADIEU TO BADWATER—TWIN FALLS—RED-FLY FISHING—A BUCK AND THE FEVER—A PLUNGE BATH—DEXTER'S PARTY—BIG QUINISECK FALLS—SCENERY—LITTLE QUINISECK FALLS—KICKING A BUCKET—SAND RAPID—A TRAIL—SHOOTING THE RAPIDS—STURGEON FARM AND STURGEON FALLS—BOBBING FOR PIKE.

TOM KING had horticultural pretensions; and, we had seen, in his carefully weeded garden, vines of water-melons and cucumbers, and other garden stuffs, in profusion of healthy flourishing. In the night, a rare August frost, a most premature spectral harbinger of winter, strayed from the far north, and nipped and blighted by its touch the whole abundant plant. In the morning, a dense fog overhung the river and obscured the sun, but ere long the warm radiance dispelled the cloud of mist as if it were snow melted away magically. It was then an unclouded heaven and a dazzling sunny day, and these were hailed by us as signs of ended rains, lowering clouds and chilling moisture, and as propitious of the favoring skies and prospering airs which would make the Menominee voyage a prolonged felicity and exhilaration. We had anticipated the descent of the river as the crowning delight of the trip.

The squaw of the cabin breakfasted us before starting. The trout of the meadow and wood, from their being the captives of a hap-hazard venture and surprise, and possibly because they were positively the last of the season to us, were specially relished. After the customary smoking and the loading of the baggage, and after Tom had got an extended furlough, for a day or two longer with us, from his better half, as neither he nor we were desirous of parting then, we launched away about nine o'clock. The river was unrippled, excepting at rapids; and just below those nearest the cabin, the other canoe was hauled from the dockage of leaves in which it was left the day previous, and the crews and the traps were divided between the two birches.

We had by this time familiarized ourselves with the peculiarities and caprices of the birch-bark, and felt at home and at ease in it, so that it was no longer a precarious or ticklish navigation to us. We knew now how to shift positions, how to stretch out or to stand erect, and had mastered the niceties of balancing ourselves and the canoe. For its ease, grace, lightness, quickness and docility of motion, the birch-bark canoe is peerless and superb among water-craft; and the Menominee we expected to find precisely the stream for canoe navigation, in its most favorable conditions.

The Twin Falls are three miles apart. While the Indians were transferring the canoes and their burden around the upper falls, we scrambled to the foot, and High ventured a cast of a brilliant red fly in the whirl, though it was quite improbable that a pike or a bass would be enticed by such a flaring gawd. Nevertheless, though all chances were against him, he whipped the water with the fly just the same, thinking if he did not win, he would at least deserve success. He saved his fly and restored the fictitious insect to the company of its fellow entomological gewgaws, in his fly-book, in its perfect integrity, for future use.

In the eddy of the lower fall, I thought the water looked as if it should be a lair of fish, and that a pickerel might be captured by one not too fastidious to try a killing bait. I rigged my tackle, and experimented with a scrap of pork on the hook, but the swine's flesh decoyed no perch, bass or pickerel, that I could grapple with hook of steel. Not even one of the abounding pitiful chubs was hungry enough to offer it a nibble. I was not long in satisfying myself that fishing in that pool was not my vocation. After pushing out and getting fairly under way, George saw a couple of deer grazing water herbage afar off. It was only a momentary vision. They vanished.

Soon again we had another sensation of deer— a splendid buck feeding in the bushes. The boys slyly stole the canoes thereaway. Pratt's ardor was enkindled; he shouldered arms, and held at the ready; the buck lifted his spreading antlers, and then dropped his nose to the grass again. George was stealthily paddling the canoe, with a fair show of stealing unawares, within shooting range. We were expecting great things of Pratt, but owing, probably, to a fluster of buck-fever, he pulled an ill-timed trigger, and though the deer was not harmed, the water was badly torn up about midway between the buck's pasturing place and ourselves. The deer bounded and ricocheted into the forest, where the woodbine twines. Pratt admitted that his premature firing was a mistake, worse even than would be that of shooting at a pigeon and killing a crow; but as the deer was just going to spring, he had to spring the trigger then, or lose the shot.

The next event, further down, was a frolic of immersion. We had turned ashore to lunch, and after dealing full justice to the spread, Bissell and Pratt were impetuously seized with a mania for a swim in the Menominee. The performance was marvelously brisk and brief. They plunged in the crystal tide with a slap-dash precipitance, but the reduction of their temperature from the frigid inclemency of the stream was so instantaneous and the effect was so glacial that with "chattering teeth and bristling hair upright," they rebounded, and plunged out, with surprising agility, Bissell rather in the lead.

Two miles further on, was the head of the portage around Big Quiniseck Falls. It was the scene of a surprise party. At about the same moment Wirt Dexter's party and our own reached the spot. With him, were Jesse Spaulding, of Chicago, and a Mr. Smith, a Bostonian lawyer, *en route* to the Brulé. Their suite and outfit were complete. They had four Indians of the Chippewa order of redmen, but they were lean, stunted-looking weaklings and manikins, aside of our brawny and robust aborigines; also, a weazened, shrivelled little mulatto cook, who seemed a scullion apart, with no affinity for his fellows of the retinue, who, in their turn, seemed to look tomahawks at the kitchen satellite, and as if they would like to strip his scalp in the first convenient bushes. The cargo was immense. Tents, cots, hair mattresses, stools, cases, barrels, kegs, crockery, valises, gun-cases, as if for a whole season's campaign. Pratt thought their equipage for roughing it was hardly complete without a piano and brussels carpet. But he is rather peculiar and high-toned, and we did not accord with him in that hypothesis. The couple of hours spent there, while both retinues were making portages of the loads, were a delightful episode in our forest adventure. Our converse was mainly on matters of the woods. Dexter has been a forest ranging Michigander, as apt in handling a trout-rod or rifle in his vacations, as he is in practice with the mysteries of Coke and Chitty in term time. There is not much about game of his native State, that which swims, goes on foot or sweeps on the wing, with which he is not familiar. His reminiscences of hunting and fishing, flavored as they were with the fragrance of Partagas, greatly entertained us.

This portage was a little more than two miles in length. It was over a rolling, hillocky surface, and though the path was not so barricaded with trunks of trees to be climbed over as most of the carries, it was yet tedious and wearisome. But at the foot of the declivity, where the trail ends, a large rock towers thirty feet above the water at its base. From this peak of rock, a splendid view bursts upon the sight, in an outlook of magnificent scenery. Off, at the right, the river avalanches down a steep incline, and pitches tumultuously far, and rolls into waves, with clouds of spray, "showering wide sleet of diamond drift and pearly hail." The water spreads and rounds out into a circular bay or basin of nearly a half mile diameter, and this is partially girded round with cliffs wooded with heaviest pageantry of forest pines and cedars, except at the further side, where the river contracts and glides away in a smooth flow or stretch between level shores and the richest of verdure.

The scene, resplendent in the setting sun, was enchanting and worthy of some master to commemorate. It was the spontaneous resolve of all the party, that the tent should be pitched on the rock, in view of scenery so picturesque and striking; and there, from the summit of the rock, and in the last rays of the sun fading and in the twilight glimmering on, we quietly enjoyed the situation with wonder and delight. We were among the splendors of primeval nature.

When the moonshine softened the landscape, and portions of it were deepened into shadow, we had time to realize how cool our elevated position was. The blankets were not quite equal to the occasion, when we retired from the expiring camp-fire and betook ourselves to the sleeping ground-spread. After their camp duties had been performed, and tired, as they must have been, from the two portages required for the transfer of canoes and luggage, Tom and Thebault had launched and paddled away in a canoe for a night-hunt of deer. They skimmed along in the shadows of the woods, creeping softly among the reeds, and though they heard and saw that the deer were afoot, the moonlight was too bright to admit of successful ambuscading.

We rose early and willingly to renew our enjoyment of the charms of the scenery. There was no satiety in the outlook around and beyond. When taking the canoes for the start, we paddled to the centre of the basin, and held up for a view from that point. Though not so grand as from the pinnacle, the scene was yet lovely. We receded from it with lingering glances. Doubtless, when means of access are opened to it, Big Quiniseek Falls will become a resort of many who make summer pilgrimages in search of health, rest and river and forest sporting. The stretch below the falls would be admirable for regattas and boating.

Three or four miles down was the base of the elevation from which, on our way up, we had our first river perspective. The Dexter party had camped there, and its Indians gave our Indians information that raspberries were to be found there. We went ashore to devastate the supposed raspberry bushes. But neither that berry nor its bush was discoverable on a pretty thorough exploration. The ascent up the steep path of sand to the plateau was compensated for in another view of the landscape, there being on this river but very rarely high-browed hills, from which a commanding prospect may be had. In consonance with the loneliness, almost desolation, of the place, a raven croaked hoarsely its ill-omened notes from a dead tree-top. On the edge of the stream a bunch of deep crimson leaves hung from their stem, quivering gently in the breeze, and reflected in the water like a burst of brilliant wavering flame.

While rounding in for the head, or trail at the head of Little Quiniseck Falls, Pratt fluttered again on espying a deer within easy range. The gun was out of harm's way, under some baggage and safely encased in its cover, tied up with knots of which at first he forgot the combination. Presently, though, the piece was uncovered, and then rummaging his pockets for caps, he, in his leisurely haste, managed to kick against a tin pail at his feet. This clatter of the tin struck an alarum at least half a mile all around, and, of course, the frightened browser leaped and cleared from sight and shot. Pratt lost the deer, but he gained a valuable experience, which satisfied him that hunting with the gun covered and uncapped, in the bottom of the boat, under a stratum of traps, was not promising of great spoil of deer or other game.

While the portaging was being attended to, we descended the rocks on the lower side and clambered along the ledges to see the cascade. Its noise apprised us that there was more than a little confusion of the waters. On the brink a large mass of rock parted the stream, and the water plunged in separate headlong cataracts of snowy white. These volumes rebound from the fall, as it were, spout up in columns or jets and, falling, mingled together and rolled away in billows, with a mist of spray and the sun

> "Caught the sparkles, and in circles,
> Purple gauzes, golden hazes, liquid mazes,
> Flung the torrent rainbow round."

These are grander cascades than that of Big Quiniseck, but the surrounding scenery, though wild, is not so grand.

After embarking and making a mile further, in the field of his vision, but far off, George discovered a couple more deer dabbling their noses in the water. But being as far-sighted as Kaquotash, they left no time for any strategy being practiced on them.

The next noted stage of the voyage was the Sand Rapid. This is the Scylla and Charybdis ordeal of the river, on account of its danger and length. The rapids are a curving sweep of three miles, and test all the skill, courage and muscle of the most experienced canoeist. The canoes could be taken through with the loads, but not with ourselves weighting them. There is a trail of two miles nearly, across to the foot of the Rapid. Before the descent of Sand Rapid begins there are short rapids around which a portage must be made. By our trailing over the short-cut, and by gaining so much start while the short carry was being made, we could reach the end of the Rapid considerably before the canoes would make the run through.

The beginning of the trail was on a long ascent

of a hill, and toward the end was a corresponding declivity, and then the course on the level was through marshes where it became obscure or lost in the grasses and brush. We groped our way out of the troublesome maze, and touched the river at the foot of the Rapid. It was a grassy bank, high and dry, and finely shaded by over-arching branches of splendid trees. We were to witness the shooting of rapids under the most exciting conditions, and, from that point, a mile of the agitated water could be seen. We waited for the canoes to come in sight.

In the meantime, Pratt and Bissell prospected among the bushes. High was resting against a colossal pine, on the shady side, confidentially giving himself away to his diary. I stretched on the grass, looking up to the dense evergreens overhead, gratefully thinking benedictions on Wirt Dexter, for the rare cigar whose luscious odors of Cuba were then mingling with the abounding forest perfumes of Michigan. All the while, the turmoiled rapids sounded their ceaseless lulling monotone of liquid music.

Soon Bissell roared out the *whoop-la* signal. We were instantly up, and on tip-toe for the scene. Away at the further end of the perspective, the canoes bounded into sight. George and Thebault manned the larger, and Tom, alone, swayed his old familiar smaller one. The birches seemed things of life that leaped and came pitching ahead, the

Indians swinging the paddle from side to side or plying the setting poles as needful to sheer off from a rock, or to hold them from rushing into a breaker, or to turn them into the winding chutes, and keep them always steady and trim from dipping or shipping water.

Alone, erect, in the middle of his canoe, his hat off and his dark hair streaming, handling the paddle, at times dropping it and snatching the setting pole, with the celerity of thought, holding her to his will, running her in the swift descent where he would, steady through a waste of seething perils, long reaching, but most swiftly shot through, when the slightest deviation from the right course would dash the frail structure to pieces or swamp her instantly, Tom was a marvel of handling, nerve and skill.

We watched them breathlessly, through the long stretching ordeal, seeming though, in the swiftness of advance, but a few moments of passage. When they safely ran in the barks to shore, with as masterly a control as that of a trained jockey reining in and bringing to bay his fiery-mettled horse, our admiration was boundless, and we greeted the daring and successful runners of the water with the loudest of huzzas.

The next stoppage was at Sturgeon farm, at Sturgeon river. That stream is the route to Hamilton lake. It is in a region noted as a stamping ground for deer. For several years Chicago parties have encamped there, and found food for powder among the "poor dappled fools of the forest," and enjoyed the abounding sport, until ammunition was all shot away, or they wearied of the excess and gore of deer. The hunting places seemed to have been regarded as a sort of private and exclusive rifle range or game preserve for their own special sport. Lake Hamilton is, practically, to the general public, nearly as little known as the Victoria Nyanza of Central Africa.

Our supplies, procured from Dickey's, had been limited, and we found it prudent to meet the contingency of short commons, or of possible delays in the voyage, to increase them. So, at the farm, we had negotiations with the supply department. From its abundant store we laid in plenteous tea, pork, syrup, flour, potatoes, butter and tobacco.

To a forest *menu* to which these would contribute, there was one delicacy needed to make it sumptuous. Our teeth were by this time set on edge for that dainty fare by frequent previous cervine evanescences. We had seen that game near and afar; had shot at it hopefully within one range and hopelessly at another distance, and, sometimes, had not shot at all, but always the deer played us the slip. These escapes, so nearly fruitions, served to tease and tantalize appetite to importunate longing. We were pledged antlers and haunches, if we could provide a dark lantern for a night hunt. This requirement we were fortunate in supplying at Sturgeon farm. We borrowed a lantern well approved for the purpose.

Making a portage around, the tents were pitched just below Sturgeon Falls, in the last glow of sunset on the water. There is Indian hearsay that pike abound in the basin here. As that fish is peculiarly voracious, it was thought there was a probable field for lively amusement in the twilight. High encouraged a trial, and captured a colossal grasshopper, for which it is known the pike has a special greed; and the fine one now his prisoner was, certainly, a most lusty and tempting specimen of that skipping family. I impaled it on my hook. I felt sure of one pike at least. It was a hard scuffle to reach a certain throwing point—a narrow ledge on a scarp of rock—and there was a preliminary tribulation of undergrowth and briars to be gone through; but I worked a way to the perch. I wagered with myself large imaginary stakes that I would take a notable pike, and rather expected my comrades were waiting to applaud the feat to the echo.

There was no reason why pike were not numerous there, and why they should not suffer themselves to be caught. In that trust, I plunged in the enticing grasshopper. But the fish were too unaccountably wary and shy to make a rush for the hook.

I placed and replaced the bait in every direction. The reputed voracity showed no sign. I began to doubt whether ravenousness was indeed a vice of the species. At any rate, the myth of grasshopper killingness was now exploded. Would a shred of pork rally the clan? A fragment of Sturgeon farm bacon was tried. But, if that had been tainted with *trichina spiralis*, it could not have been more cautiously shunned. The nutritious grasshopper and the unctuous pork proved equally fallacious.

I was at my wits end, and further, was convinced that even the existence there of pike was a hallucination, and thought in future I would treat all Indian tradition with contempt. Feeling myself a victim of misplaced confidence, I swore off from even the bare imagination of pike forever, scrambled perilously from off the rock, and scathingly through the briar hedge and alder thicket, back to the camp.

How mercilessly I might have been bantered and twitted on my egregious water-haul, I was luckily unaware, from the fact that, just then, attention was diverted in another direction. Across the basin, in the *chiar-oscuro* of the deepening twilight, was a figure of a deer shadowly outlined. George slipped a canoe silently across, to try a shot, and everybody held his peace and watched for the result. But noiselessly though the birch-bark thitherward stole its course, the deer was too vigilant to be surprised, and it vanished into the evening shades.

## CHAPTER VIII.

NIGHT HUNT—VENISON—SPLENDID ANTLERS—TOM KING'S PARTING—A LOOK FOR A DEER—A FAWN SLAIN—COMPUNCTION—PEEMBINWUN RAPIDS AND RUNNING THEM—A MARCH STOLEN--BISSELL'S BUCK-HORNS—HOME LONGING—WHITE RAPIDS—ANOTHER PARTING—A BROOKLET TROUTED IN—PIKE RIVER—INDIAN MAIDEN—WAUSAUKA BEND—HIGH'S DEVOIRS TO THE GENTLE SEX—MOSQUITOES.

THE Indians intended doing their part towards verifying the promise of deer. They organized a lantern hunt, and expected, before the moon arose, or was high, to accomplish the mission. They trimmed the wick, rubbed up the gun, fresh loaded and capped it, and parleyed briefly but earnestly, in their native tongue, and in their air and actions evinced a serious purpose of business. They now had the lantern, whose use they had declared was an almost certain gage of success, and their own credit was pledged, from the start down the river, to diet us with venison on the trip. They now meant to make good their promise, and assured us that from deer resorts in the vicinage, they would return to the camp with at least one carcass.

George, with the gun and lantern, and Thebault, with the paddle, slipped the canoe quietly down the river in the dark. Tom King crept under the other upturned canoe in front of the fire, and curled up for slumber, and quickly slipped into happy hunting grounds in the realm of sleep and dreams. We prated and speculated on the results. The query whether Diogenes, on his lantern hunt, ever found his man, which sometimes used to be a school-boy quiz, was never a quirk or conceit as interesting and speculative to men of our stomach, as was now the conundrum whether Kaquotash's lantern would prove a means of success.

A deer was the necessary complement of our wants. It omitted, all the voyage, thence to the end, would be bound in shallows and in miseries. Before we were asleep the report of the gun in the distance told us a hopeful tale. Another shot followed in a brief interval. We were content, then, to wrap our blanket covering around us and lie down for the night, with our last waking thoughts of venison, and with assurance of a morning reality of deer.

At sunrise, while the shadows of sleep were yet on us, the boys rounded in the canoe, and roused us with a cheering loud *whoop-la*. We quickly opened our eyes, turned out, and hailed the natives with acclamations, as we saw the carcass of a fat-haunched doe stretched on the grass. The stripping of the hide, and the dissection necessary for packing away and for the present cooking fire, were processes that nimble fingers and a keen knife soon accomplished. The breakfast was a princely banquet to us.

While Thebault was cleaning the platters, all at once he signaled us with a finger pointing across the basin. There, in plain view, was a magnificent buck, with lordly horns, pasturing in the grass, raising his head gracefully to look around, and dropping it again to the herbage. The sight was one to move even an old hunter's blood. Tom and George instantly launched and stepped in a canoe, crouched down and noiselessly sped it to and behind a petty wooded island which was enough a cover to mask their movement. Tom landed, and, cat-like, crept stealthily to a good position, and within easy shooting distance, where the "fat burgher of the woods" still stood feeding. Tom poised himself and the gun. We stood motionless, waiting the shot, and heard Tom snap both caps—the gun missed fire! The click, of course, startled the buck, and, with a lofty spring, and in a great agitation of bushes, and with an erected tail, he bounded into the distance. Even Indian passivity gave way, and both George and Tom uttered a cry of disappointment. Both pronounced him a noble fellow, and

Tom's highest praise of him was that his horns would weigh thirty pounds.

This incident was Tom King's last in our service. He left us here to return home afoot. In the woods, on the stream, in the camp and in his own cabin, he had been faithful, pleasant and valuable. There was not a little of the white man's ways, mingled with a good deal of the red man's, in him. He is ready, like most of his race, to lend a hand at any casual thing that he may find, but is mostly a trapper. He makes Marquette the trading place for his pelts, and makes journeys there in winter on the ice and snow of the Michigami river. The parting hand we gave him was warm with the friendliest adieu. No one of us will soon forget the Menominee, Tom King, of Badwater.

The first shot of the night hunt we heard, was at a deer on the river bank. The Indians thought the animal was disabled, if not killed, and would probably be found in the woods. The deer brought in was shot on the edge of a small lake. The boys remained there, sleeping in the canoe. After leaving the camp, on our way down, a landing was made for a search at the place where the deer of the night before was thought to have been shot. The brush, thickets of bushes and trunks of fallen timber, were so nearly impenetrable, to us, at least, that it seemed a mystery how even an unwounded buck could get his crown of antlers and himself through the compact wilderness.

This density of undergrowth and *debris* of timber are found everywhere, but for all that, the flying deer vanishes with unaccountable certainty and speed. The Indians had trouble to move about, but scoured the fastnesses all around. We struck on a profusion of red raspberries, near the bank, and vigorously raided the bushes while the search for the suppositional deer was going on. The Indians must have befooled themselves, after all, as they found no trace of the deer, wounded or dead. Pratt and myself, with George, went on in the advance.

Pratt's time at last came to witch us with a feat of marksmanship. A doe and her twin fawns were pacing down a partially cleared bank ahead, not seeing us. Around a bend we stole a quick, close turn and surprise on them as they were lapping the water in the edge of the stream. Before they could top the steep bank, for which they sprang, the gun was ready, just then, with fatal accuracy, and shattered the hind leg of one of the fawns, when it fell back and reeled into a shallow pool formed by a tongue of sand, and helplessly struggled in the water. George leaped ashore and grappled it. Pratt stepped out and towards it. The woeful creature turned its head to Pratt, looking him in the face, and bleated piteously, as if imploring him to help or spare it. George dispatched it with a merciful thrust of a knife in its throat.

The crying, quivering fawn, crimsoning the sand,

was a spectacle recalling the similar one of the wounded deer in the forest of Arden:

> "The wretched animal heaved forth such groans
> That their discharge did stretch his leathern coat
> Almost to bursting; and his big round tears
> Coursed one another down his innocent nose
> In piteous chase."

Pratt, like the melancholy Jaques, was disposed to sigh over the sobbing creature; the spectacle so touched his tender and sympathetic nature that, in a mood of compassion and compunction, he solemnly vowed himself against any future merely sportive or needless slaughter of the innocents.

We passed all along through the finest and loveliest river and forest scenery. The stream was broad and smooth, and a delicious air tempered the radiance of the sun, so that gliding in easy and gentle motion over the water, with the senses all in reposeful harmony, was like the calm and soft lapsing into sleep. At a little cleft in the solid wall of verdure was a solitary white man lying on the ground with a rifle pitched against a tree, just at hand, on a lonely watch for deer. The place was a deer crossing, a run-way or path to the water, to which they repair for swimming over. Many of them are frequently ambushed in this way, during the season, when they are migrating.

Not far below him was an Indian encampment, or bark cabin, where venison for winter was being smoked, and deerskins were drying in the sun. A graded infant school of papooses seemed to have been turned out to play when we passed, while a couple of curs yelped at us an unfriendly clamor. At noon we reached Peembinwun rapids. They were an ugly and hazardous rush and tumult of waters. The canoes were brought to; the Indians got out and took a survey, and held an earnest and considerate pow-wow. They thought they might venture to run the canoes through, if partially lightened of the load of ourselves and what baggage we could carry around.

Each of us gripped our blankets and valises and, in not very light marching order, filed along the portage. The lighter canoe went safely through the turmoil. But the ordeal was more doubtful and perilous for the larger and more loaded birch-bark, as both skill and danger were involved in the headlong passage. We were eager to witness the homestretch of the exciting run. Our point of view was the brow of a little cliff overlooking the scene. We saw the craft let loose, and sweeping on among the tossing breakers, guided by incredibly quick changes of the paddle, or by sheering with the pole, and shooting madly ahead, and swiftly, like a weaver's shuttle, all through, but in safety, into the calm waters below. We huzzaed the boys with a will.

It was only a short time after leaving that place, that an inconsiderate deer was seen nibbling grass in the water's edge. As it was a short-horned buck, and Pratt's vow of compassionate forbearance only applied to fawns, it was no act of perfidy to himself to shoot the heedless quadruped then before him, if he could. He, therefore, mobilized his forces for the occasion. The deer must have been as deaf as a post, or the victim of some inscrutable delusion or optical infirmity, else George could not have sneaked a direct march to within forty yards distance from it. As it stood with its whole broadside fully exposed, in point blank range, a conspicuous target, Pratt himself must have been egregiously wild and random in his gunnery, not to have smitten the deer with a hail of buckshot. So, in fact, he did effectually pepper and perforate its leathern coat, so that the deer dropped wounded into the water, where it struggled desperately to regain its feet.

George ran the canoe to it, sprang out, and with a cut-throat jab of his knife, ended its respiratory functions forever. The readiness with which the Indians flayed off the skin, was suggestive of the neatness and dispatch of the scalp-stripping process for which the untamed savage has a natural devilish proclivity and historic repute. A haunch was carved off for venison steaks, and the rest of the carcass was left there to feast the minks and crows of the woods.

Pratt had now fairly won his spurs as a deer-slayer, and being once more a little scrupulous about needless bloodshedding, was ready to hand over the armament and munitions to Bissell, who was more than willing to undertake the gory business. He was not much of a field sportsman, and had yet to realize his first flurry of buck-fever. He wanted to try his hand. To shoot one deer only would be glory and fame enough for him.

Bissell had very wisely forethought that, in case of failure to hack a pair of horns from the bleeding front of a buck of his own slaying, as a souvenir of the woods to be taken home to excite the admiration of his friends, it might be well to take the hint from a frequent trick of luckless fishers who come home laden with messes caught in the fish market with a price. So he had provided at Dickey's a jolly front of antlers, which had long hung seasoning among the cobwebs of the cabin rafters, and sent it by Evanson's team to Marinette for expressage to Chicago.

A rage to kill just one deer is not uncommon with verdant men-at-arms. There is a story of one of these irrepressible fellows, who was one of Burton C. Cook's party making a tour of the woods. He carried his rifle constantly on the *qui vive* for the imminent deer. The solitary one that materialized on the entire round of the trip, as if by the wind of fortune blown to mortal doom in the apparent jaws of destruction, cantered without scath, and close past the very clump of bushes where Verdant Venator, just then disarmed, had lain down on the grass to snooze.

By this time Pratt and Bissell were affected with premonitory symptoms of home-fever, by reason of supposed exigencies of business. Though they loved our gentle, dreamy and tardy voyaging not less, they favored home-tending rapid momentum more. High and I were still untired of the woods and the stream, and would fain prolong the canoeing and tenting to the extent of the most leisurely and tardy return. By the camp fire at night we sat in sober council over the matter, and puffed a great deal of smoke during the session, but we neither befogged their wits with the smoke, nor was our logic potent enough to convince them that we understood the demands of their business better than themselves, or to change what had become a foregone conclusion.

Home being the word, the next thing was to arrange the details, as to a division of the flotilla, of supplies and of Indian service. As there was no peremptory spirit or any positive ultimatum on either side, a result was speedily reached. Early in the morning the camp was in motion, and the matin repast soon prepared and dispatched. To give our parting comrades a good send-off, we embarked at the same time to consort them as far as White Rapids.

There, in the smaller canoe, and with George as

swinger of the paddle, Bissell and Pratt stowed themselves and their belongings. Bissell figuratively said that there was not a dry eye in the party. There were no visible ocular effects, but we all felt some flutter of the heart, some twitching of the lips and some swell in the throat, when the good-bye was spoken and the parting hand in hand was clasped. It was a parting we could well have spared. We sat on the bank watching them. As they receded, they waved us with their white cambrics one last adieu, and then another, until they vanished in the far-down offing.

White Rapids, so called from a reach of shallow, white-capped rapids, is a settlement of a Chippewa populace, and of a half-dozen cabins, with small natural meadows on both shores, greenly bordering the frothy and brawling turbulence of the river. Excepting New York farm, this meadowy and disforested acreage was more typical, apparently, of Christianity, civilization and agriculture, than anything yet seen along the Menominee.

A half mile back, there is an infinitesimal brook, spirally lengthening through a patch of meadow, and running into an impenetrable wood. Paltry as it is, there is a current Indian tradition of its being a trout stream. High thinks wherever there flows such a brook or rill, he must have a throw there, and to pass by a streamlet with trout in it, even were they but minnows of trout, without making its acquaintance, even briefly, would be a dereliction for which he could not easily forgive himself.

Thebault led the way to the petty stream. It looked as if it would be trouting under difficulties to experiment in it with the fly. The grasses almost smothered it; osiers and branches overhung it, and there was an interlock, often, of brush on the bottom and through it, and it was all one could do to cast a line anywhere. At the hazard of utterly demoralizing his rod, and of his eyes being scratched out, or of his clothes being slit into rags, High pushed in wherever he could thrust his nose through the hindrances, and seemed to enjoy the vexations of such angling. However, he so efficiently wielded the rod, that in not much more than an hour's worrying in the thickets he had whisked out nineteen handsome trout.

I thought that in this wayside or chance diversion he evinced greatly more of the higher skill and qualities of an expert troutsman than he did in the canoe fishing on the Brulé, where the elbow-room was free and the throwing clear. These trout, it is true, put on the scales, would not tell a large figure in a total of pounds, but I fancied High was rather proud of this achievement, and that in the way, if not of weight, yet of patience, art and skill, these nineteen trifles made enough of a wonder of exploit to show Thebault and myself how angling thus was to "strive with things impossible, yea, get the better of them," as in fact it seemed to be.

Pike river comes in not far below White Rapids. An Indian cabin stands there. We thought we could there hear news of Stockton's party, and so turned ashore to interview the natives of the habitation. We all of us started up the path leading to it. A ferocious, long-haired, large dog was lying in front of the door, in the sun, snapping wickedly at flies or fleas. Thebault, as dragoman, took the lead, we following, with our eyes carefully fixed on the dog, which, however, was so exclusively devoted to his petty tormentors that he scarcely noticed us. We entered the domicile. The inmates were female, except possibly a swaddled papoose, clinging, affrighted, around the maternal neck. After once starting, their squaw gift of speech was quite equal in fluency and copiousness to that of the most gifted of their Christian sisters.

Our inquiry as to the Stockton party was satisfied in learning that it had passed the day before into Pike river in good plight. But the conversation took, evidently, a wider scope, and our interpreter probably was doing the agreeable on his own account. One of the gentle savages was girlish, and quite comely in the face, with raven dark hair, "like the sweep of a swift wing in vision," though the rather bulbous figure and ponderous size, and a foot that would "bend a blade of grass or shake the downy blow-ball from his stalk," were not types of feminine grace or models of art. But, withal, this belle of the lodge or wigwam would not be unattractive, even beyond the pale of Indian paganism.

A picture of more grace than the Indian maiden was a beautiful fawn standing on the bank at Wausauka bend, calmly looking us in the face. Thebault tried to scare it by motioning and shouting, but it only trotted off a few paces and faced us again, as if lost or confused. The spotted innocent was entirely out of harm's way from us, as the gun that the "round haunches gor'd" was then on a forced march to Marinette.

As we turned the bend at Wausauka, we swept into the prospect of a fine large spreading meadow or sward, and a little on, in the river edge of the landscape were two white tents with a covered wagon, some grazing horses and a good deal of a day's washing hung out to dry. These were signs of civilization. We bore down at once for the camp. Our coming appeared to have brought out of the tents three or four women and children, on a surprise and with a curiosity equal to our own.

To us, this appearance of ladies in that out-of-the-way place was like a happy vision burst on us out of the heavens. We were ready to echo Jaffier's fervid tribute to woman, or at least, to recall it, that angels are painted fair to look like her; she has in her all we believe of heaven; and we had been brutes without her. Under the inspiration of this or a similar chivalrous sentiment, High thought it his duty, regarding, for the moment, these ladies as personating, or typifying, the sex in general, to offer them his homage.

The gallant chevalier stepped ashore for that purpose. He was mindful enough of the difference between woman in the abstract and in the particular to move a little further and out of the way to make up to the fairest one of the sirens. Knowing very well the sensibility of the sex to the charms of scenery, he attempted to steal a march into her good graces through this weak point by the delicate topographical observation, conveyed in the blandest manner: "This is a beautiful camping place, madam." There was nothing extravagant or far-fetched in that remark, and the deportment of High was admirable.

Whether the lady felt that it was the crowning glory of a true woman to be the admiration and happiness of *one* rather than the toast, or the cynosure of any "vagrom men" that might come roving along there in canoes, without letters of introduction or testimonials of character; or, whether the offense was in addressing her as madame and not mademoiselle, she, at all events, received and responded to High's winning amenities of speech and manner with a giggle and snicker of derision, and majestically strode back into the tent. So did her sisters and her cousins and her aunts. This ended the deportment business, shattered the Jaffier ideal into smithers, and settled High. He retired in as good order as he could, considering the sudden demoralization, and asked me if I could see anything in *that* remark to laugh at. He did not think I could, and, I owned, I could not.

The only suggestion I could offer him for the unaccountable disdain of the lady he had picked out as the particular one angels were painted fair to look like, was that the apparel of our party generally, and of some of it in particular, was in a condition of seediness and decrepitude that may have marked us in her mind as tramps or fellows no better than we should be. We learned that the ladies were of a party from Menominee, encamping there, the gentlemen of which were then out hunting.

# CHAPTER IX.

SANITARY MATTERS--DAVIS' PAIN-KILLER—THE RELAY HOUSE AGAIN—FARLIN'S PARTY--LYING IN THE SHADE—UPPER TWIN ISLAND—LAST CAMP AND ITS DISCOMFORTS—THE LOWER MENOMINEE—AT MENOMINEE—END OF THE TRIP.

THE river turns on itself at Wausauka, forming a long promontory three miles around, by canoe, but across its base, by portage, only a few rods. We preferred the three miles of ease and languor on the water-way to a short portage, and when we had made the run, we landed and crowned the top of the steep bank with our camp and tent for the night. This was on one of the borders of the open or clearing of Wausauka, and commanded a fine view of it and of the river.

We found we had placed ourselves at the mercy of the most ravenous mosquitoes of the whole trip. The comparatively moderate skirmish line that attended our landing was reinforced, from time to time, by swarms from a distance, until we were beclouded with the biting legions. We smudged our faces and hands with oil and tar, and repeating this was a principal branch of the business carried on at night in the tent.

So far we had had a clean bill of health, and the sanitary condition had been superb. But at Wausauka promontory camp, High fancied he was out of sorts. The entire stock of medicines at command consisted of one vial of Davis' pain-killer, and one vial of aperient powders, so of course the choice of remedies was limited. He thought the pain-killer would "yank" him about right. I thought it did. A few drops of it in warm water told the story. If its internal effects were to be judged from the puckering of the mouth and wryness of face, his true inwardness must have been in a state of lively commotion. Its effect, however, was happy, and restored High to his customary hygienic condition and cheerfulness.

We were sped onwards gently and steadily by Thebault, counting the hours, not that they came too slowly, but that they were, one by one, bringing us nearer to the end of the voyage. When we came to the Relay House landing, near the hut of the priest-hunter, we moved, or rather drew out on the bank our canoe, and tramped the half-mile way to the Relay House. We had, the day before, seen a fleet of four canoes being poled up the river, and learned now that Farlin's party had passed there, by team, on the route we had taken, to Sturgeon farm, to go into camp at Hamilton Lake. This party was a nimrod party more than a trout-rod party, and was to devote itself much more to using bullets than to recreation with the fly.

The Relay House was quite empty and silent. Its few inmates were off in the fields, and its appearance was very different from that of the rainy evening our party housed there. Even the logman's hut was left by the clergyman to its solitude, and the scene was little like that of our night at the hostelry. Two miles below we hauled to for lunch, at a grassy bank, though the shade was meagre.

As all the hurry and home-fever passed off with Pratt and Bissell, we had time enough on our hands, and were trying to take our ease for the remainder of the short trip. We found shade enough for a siesta; the breeze was lively, waving the grasses and foliage into woodland music and roughing the stream into silver wavelets. We readily enough dropped into slumber, and only roused when the signal of the lunch was given. We awoke from a siesta or any sleep that reached to a meal hour, by a sort of self-acting impulse, like that of an alarm clock set to strike at an alloted hour, when a repast was set out. Foresters and campers train themselves to, or acquire, this sort of automatic waking up to answer demands of the stomach.

After the refreshing doze and the lunch, and on the voyage being again resumed, we had the almost daily pillar of cloud following in the wake, which shaded us from the sun at first, but, in its thickening and darkening, ominously prognosticated a heavy rain. We were just enough ahead of the masses of cloud, to reach a point eligible, but, at all events, necessary for setting the tent in a field or clearing opposite the end of Upper Twin Island. The rain did us the service and favor of holding off until the tent was stretched and pegged down, and very soon after the showers fell copiously for a time; and, in an interval, partly of entire cessation and partly of subsiding into a sprinkle, the cooking fire was kept barely alive long enough to afford us the customary draught of tea, and some other of the staples, for supper.

We had not more than finished our evening refection when the rain began pouring in torrents, leaking through the tent, and running in from one side in little rills at our feet. Thebault scoured the adjacency, where was an Indian cabin, to hunt timber or pieces of wood to support or prop up the blanket quarters out of a puddle. He confiscated some clapboards from somewhere, and by laying them on the ground we improvised a water-proof bedstead for the final sleep in the woods.

To add to the misery and discomfort of the situation, the mosquitoes of all the country—at least of more than one township—semed to swarm in for shelter from the rain. They were rapacious, and thirsted for nothing less than all the blood of all the party. The air was close, damp and sultry, and all these, with the constant flashing of lightning and frequent peals of thunder, far into the night, made our tent anything but a pavilion of ease, rest and deep sleep. We were only sixteen miles from Marinette. We had heard the six o'clock steam-whistle of the mills there. That sound was the knell or signal of our ending life in the tent and in the woods. The memories of the last camp were disagreeable ones. Rain, heat, thunder, lightning, mosquitoes, sleeplessness, in aggravating combination, served to make it almost a night of horrors. The scenery of the river and all the charm of navigating it end at Twin Islands. From thence to the mouth was a monotony of barrenness and almost waste, the timber having been long since stripped off.

We reached Menominee at noon. The vacation ramble ended there; canoeing on the streams and tenting in the forests, our open air life, were to be, thence, only memories; but with us, memories always golden and abiding!

# CHAPTER X.

SECOND BRULE EXCURSION—NEW ROUTE—ARTHUR T. JONES—NEW GUIDES—PREVIOUS ARRANGEMENTS—W. H. STENNETT—REPUBLIC—THE MICHIGAMI—UNEASY LYING—STORES—CIRCULATING LIBRARY—TWO KISSES—A BEAR AHEAD—TROUTING AND CHUBS—TALKING SHOP—A METEOROLOGICAL-LEGAL CONTROVERSY—THE EARLY RISER—BROOKS—A STATUESQUE GROUP—DUCK-FEVER—A NIGHTHUNT—FIRST BLOOD—HUZZA FOR DENISON.

A SECOND Brulé river excursion was arranged. The members of it were High, Pratt, the writer, and Franklin Denison, also a Chicago lawyer. A route different from that traced in the previous pages was chosen. This was to afford novelty, greater variety of scenery and a traverse of further and wider regions. The railway connections were the Chicago & Northwestern through Marinette to Negaunee, thence the Marquette, Houghton and Ontonagon Railway to Humboldt, and thence a short branch to Republic, on the Michigami river, where are the great iron mines of that name.

The canoes of the previous voyage, the Dickey and Tom King, had been laid by at Marinette, in the care of Arthur T. Jones, the freight and ticket agent of the North-Western Railway at that place, and as a sort of pledge committed to his guardianship, had been carefully and safely kept in all their integrity, ready on call for immediate service. This gentleman is himself an expert and devotee both of rod and gun, and is, as well as W. H. Stennett, the General Passenger Agent of the Chicago & North-Western Railway, at Chicago, a cyclopedia of information on all matters relating to sport, either hunting or fishing, and the routes leading to the regions of sport in Wisconsin and upper Michigan, so many of which are traversed or reached, from Chicago, by the North-Western Railway and its connections, and, also, relating to the necessary equipment and the means of supplying it. Like other cyclopedias, these gentlemen are free and liberal of their information to all who may choose to consult them.

To Mr. Jones' kindly and accommodating civility, and to his intelligent foresight in our behalf, we were much and gratefully indebted for the success and pleasure which, it will be seen, attended our excursion. Particularly by his judicious action, in pre-concert with us, we were provided, in advance, with a splendid retinue of guides. These were, the reader's acquaintance of the previous pages, Mitchell Thebault, David Kaquotash, a younger brother of the George Kaquotash of the former Brulé party, and a veteran in woodcraft, Paul Thebault, brother of Mitchell Thebault, and Joe Dixon, the two latter half-breeds. We knew from Mr. Jones that these, our new acquaintances, were trusty, willing and hearty in such service, and that they were experienced in woods and life in the woods, from having traversed our intended route, as well as other directions in the wilderness, with parties prospecting timber lands, or with locators or surveyors of land, or with parties, like our own, in pursuit of vacation sport and recreation. In the robust and athletic frames of these auxiliaries we could, at a glance, foresee all the muscle and endurance requisite for the service for which they were engaged. The canoes, with David in charge, had been forwarded by Mr. Jones to Republic a day in advance. The other three guides joined us at Marinette.

On a clouded August afternoon, the party and its outfit reached Republic, and first touched the Michigami river.

Around the hill, a mile below the village, on the brink of the river, was the first encampment. The water-works for supplying the mines, with the rumbling machinery, was close at hand. The situation was not delightful. The dull, leaden sky made it look, and the damp air made it feel, much less than pleasing. The temperature reminded us of a Chicago November, but nothing at all of August dog-days.

Even under these inauspicious conditions, Pratt was almost buoyant, and Denison well-nigh irrepressible. In fact, both of them thought they might prelude a little to get their hands in, one with the rod and one with the gun. The prospect for game or fish at that point was wholly unpromising. Pratt, with his fly-rod, struck an attitude on the bank, and presently snatched out an ignoble chub. This instantly chilled his ardor, and he promptly betook himself to camp for some other more satisfying resource. Denison, equipped with his fire-arms, ranged about in search of anything on foot or wing, and worked his way to the east of us, among the bushes. He did not wholly waste his time or ammunition. He put a solitary partridge to death and blowed a chattering kingfisher to its kingdom come. High and myself tediously busied ourselves in doing nothing.

Our first night encampment was not delightful or soothing. The air was very damp and chilling, and we shivered as it swept freely and moistly about us. When we had retired, sleep was won only after long and toilsome pursuit. Sleepers on hair mattresses, feather pillows and in chambers, could not, all at once, fall into the different somniferous conditions of a blanket bed, with boots or satchel for bolster, *terra firma* for bedstead, and an airy tent for dormitory. Of course, a discipline of restlessness was a natural preliminary to our first sleep. One of the party referred to a vulgar calumny of many of the unregenerate, that lawyers find lying on any or either side no trouble at all, and observed that he had been lying on one side, and then lying on the other side, most of the night, and the lying was anything but easy, and certainly was not his forte. Probably this was meant as a joke, but at all events it was received as fact and in silence.

Another of the party, in a reflective mood before sleep, could discern from what seemed unpropitious signs, only an unpromising outlook ahead. Much of the glowing native hue of the resolution with which he set out on the expedition, had considerably sicklied over with a pale and cheerless cast of thought. He sang small and in the penitential strain of a miserere. However, with the dawn of morning and the lifting of the dense fog, which in the night thickly encompassed us, and in the glowing sunshine, the situation and prospect changed their seeming, and the perspective of the mind's eye brightened into harmony with the radiance of the sky.

The night's experience taught me that additional blanketing was essential. My Chicago blankets were too light. Fortunately the Iron Company's store had a stock of these goods of all qualities. I made my way to the village and procured a pair, heavy with the fleeces of many sheep, and suitable for regions more Arctic than these. High, who was to be my fellow of the couch, seeing the comfort lying in their folds, welcomed their arrival in the tent with a smile of benignity. They would contribute to the warmth of feeling between us.

The forenoon was spent by the Indians in overhauling the canoes which had not swam the water for a year, and there were seams to be pegged up and leaks to be pitched. They handled the craft delicately, in fact lovingly, as if they were things of life endeared to them. We took account of stock, of the collective outfit, of our eight pairs of blankets, which, when spread, were to be slept on, and when rolled into bundles would be sat on, of our two ponchos, of our valises, of our tackle. There were Denison's gun-case and his caisson, in which his fixed ammunition and deadly missiles were carried.

The contents of the baskets and valises were curiously miscellaneous. In the way of hygienic precaution there was a whole pocket pharmacy of homœopathic tincts, pills and powders. Pratt was our professor of the theory and practice of medicine, and actual medical adviser and dispenser. For miasmatic localities there was Kentucky old crow, some sour mash for probable malarial effects, and, as a general tonic, or catholicon, to be used as an extraordinary remedy (consult High's "Extraordinary Remedies,") there was Hennesey Cognac (1865).

By exercise of a liberal foresight, abundant fare was provided to feed the mind and meet any reasonable intellectual avidity of the party. In fact there was a circulating library in the valises. The catalogue included three or four of Jules Verne's inventions, Lakeside edition, ten cents, "Joshua Haggard's Daughter," "Weavers and Weft," "Christie Johnson," "Two Destinies," "Heaps of Money," "The American Senator," and a few other brown-tint, paper-covered novelistic obscurities. It will be perceived that this was the very lightest intellectual marching baggage.

Supposing for myself that the merest nut-shell, as it were, of literature, would be enough for the mental sustentation of trouters and canoeists, and as a resource for a rainy day, I had brought Walton's "Complete Angler" as my own sole reading. It was chosen from a principle or sense of congruity. Its theme accorded with our programme, which was piscatorial, and it would seem that the reading for the occasion should relate to the aim and spirit of the occasion. For instance, Denison's speciality being that of hunting more than of angling, I fancied his literary researches would relate to the natural history of the regions to be traversed, or to the science of gunning and projectiles. But his bookish humor was not for subjects of gunpowder or zoology.

I had my opinion of Denison when I saw the sentimental gunner stretch out languidly on his blanket spread, and fall a-sighing over Hawley Smart's love tale of "Two Kisses." The title-page motto of that romance of tender affection, "Methinks no wrong it were if I should steal from those two melting rubies, one poor kiss," settled it as to the insidious and inflammatory tenor of that story of lips and love, and for what his literary mouth watered. It was rather a wonder that he, an off-shoot of Plymouth rock and a scion of a devout Puritan ancestry, should rapturize over a perilous romance, whose very front legend or key-note was an incentive and lure to kissing kleptomania.

There was a rumor of a great bear ranging the country down the river. This bruin would be notable food for any man's powder, and test any sportsman's grit and mettle. Thinking forearming should follow forewarning, Denison ransacked his caisson for the right cartridges, carefully wiped and oiled his gun, and whetted his belt-knife to an extra savage edge. He seemed to challenge a mortal encounter, and to look the defiance " bring on your bears, now!"

There was nothing we were more willing to part withal than with our water-works encampment. At two o'clock the flotilla was ready to cast off, and turning our backs on the forbidding scene, we soon glided on the current of the Michigami into the wilderness. Denison and Pratt, with the armament, were in the advance canoe which David paddled. We followed in its wake, and in short time saw our consort vessel rounding towards an expanse of high grass in a bordering swamp. Before we discovered the cause of turning shoreward, the shot gun and David's rifle were simultaneously discharged, and we saw a doe leap out of the grass and dash off in confusion, and presently spring in the air again, but finally disappear in the reedy jungle. A search was made for the wounded animal, but it had limped or dragged itself beyond reach. Only four miles further on was seen another deer browsing in the reeds, and two shots were aimed at and wounded it, for it was seen to stagger for a moment bewildered or stunned, but on exploration by the Indians, only some stains of blood, but not the bleeding deer itself, were found.

We then advanced a long stretch of smooth water, in a very solitude of calm. Pratt's piscatory instinct was incited on reaching a tiny brooklet that quietly found way into the river, and though it is generally supposed that the Michigami is not a trout stream at all, to Pratt's eye favorable conditions for trouting were not wanting. So the canoe was laid in at the brook's mouth for him to try a cast. Almost at the touch of his fly on the water there was a rise, and Pratt had the credit of taking the first and precursory trout. High's eye glistened. Denison disarmed. Their rods were quickly put in order. All of them rapidly cast in their hackles, and the trout jumped lively for a half-hour. During this time, thirty of them were brought to grief.

By general consent the trout simultaneously subsided, and gave way to the exasperating chubs, which began just as soon to betray their impertinent voracity. The rods were promptly disjointed, and speedy departure followed. Denison was so disgusted at the onset of the chubs, that the first one which tackled his fly was flung high and far on the road to Jericho, in the woods, by the pitiless vigor of his backward swing.

A few rods on we turned ashore, to camp. While the tent was being set, I threw in a bass-line with a chub on the hook. A two-pound perch happened to be swimming around on the lookout for an evening meal, and just in the mood and at the instant for a greedy dash at the tempting bait. The perch was captured and landed.· That satisfied my yearning for sport. The encampment was high and at a bend. The river is tortuous, and turning bends was so common that Denison had a lively business on his hands in keeping trace of the points and courses with his pocket compass.

Our supper was a banquet of trout. These being the first of our catch, and rather a surprise, imparted, perhaps, a keener relish to the dish. In the after-supper lounge and idling, Denison again, silently and apart, meditated on the theme of the kiss and melting ruby lips, and pursued the tender story of the lovers in the novel. Should Hawley Smart weave other amorous tales of osculation, Frank is hardly the man to suffer any of his favorite hand-books of the law, such as "Daniell's Chancery Practice," to absorb him from the enjoyment of such affecting memoirs.

High and Pratt entertained themselves and me by fishing over again their previous years' angling on the Megalloway, Parmachene Lake and in the wilds of northern Maine, and in the smoke of our log-heap fire azurely wavering above us, recalled the memories of Whipple's roaring camp-fires on that trip. When the twilight deepened obscurity over the pages, and he lost sight of the lovers in the shadows, Denison laid away his book, and found vent for his inappeasable vitality in practising gunnery. He delivered a random volley at a bat that wheeled about in circles round us, in the waning light, and then also scattered a canister charge at a fearless muskrat that was cutting triangular ripples across the stream.

When we were retired to the tent, it was formally and solemnly agreed that no one should introduce or talk shop, under penalty of a ducking. This was partly because three of us learned gentlemen were too many for Pratt, who was not learned, and who, though knowing little about lands, tenements and hereditaments, except the rents and profits thereof, was not familiar with the legal mysteries relating to them, as expounded in Coke or Cruises' Digest, and beause we ought not to worry him and ourselves with the vain subtleties and quiddities of the law, and because on any question started we could never agree, and there were sure to be three different opinions.

Later in the evening, the party thought I rather transgressed the rule. I referred to a curious case in Iowa, where a meteorlite fell on a granger's land. A dispute about this worthless product of the upper regions was about as meritorious and profitable, one would think, as the suit about the shadow of the donkey which Demosthenes related to the gaping mob of Athens. But still the subtlety and learning of some of the pundits of the profession were sharply exercised on the question whether it belonged, by law, to the finder, by right of discovery, or to the owner of the land, as an accession. This reference was imputed to me as a misdemeanor plainly within the interdict of shop. I protested that it was a meteorological rather than a legal matter. But the preposterous wiseacres solemnly gave judgment against me. But they, Denison *dissentiente*, graciously suspended the execution of the sentence of ducking, at least until we should reach warmer water below.

The Republic blankets made High and me bless our stars for the thoughtful prescience which had added them to our sleeping kit. They were needed. The air at night was frost-like, and after High got up and grubbed out a protruding root over which he had been sometime unrestfully turning, as on a pivot, and after the others in their blankets moderated their snoring, we fell into our first slumbering in the woods, and it was peaceful and deep.

Pratt was our morning harbinger, and peep o' day boy. He liked to see what envious streaks did lace the severing clouds in yonder east, and the jocund day stand tiptoe on the misty mountain, hill or tree tops, or whatever height, as Romeo saw them. Whether the eyelids of the morn, or of Pratt were first opened, was always an open question. The Indians, even, lagged in their snore after he rose—not long, though, for he soon roused and bestirred them to diligence around the wood-heap kitchen range, that breakfast might come soon apace. While the cooking was being attended to, he and Denison navigated themselves to the little stream where the trout were found, to try again

"The fond credulity
Of silly fish, which, worldling-like, still look
Upon the bait, but never on the hook."

They returned with the inglorious trophy of one trout apiece.

We broke camp about nine o'clock. A porcupine, looking like, and as still as, a bump on a log, was seen sprawled out on a half sunken and fallen tree in the water. Denison leveled dead at it, and wounded it. We drew up, and Thebault despatched it with his paddle, after its making fight. A mile or two below, we trailed around rapids which were passable by the canoes only when lightened. We almost lost the trail, and jogged ahead slowly, over logs, through bushes and branches, a longish, weary route. We had our rods and baskets, for the Indians said there were trout below.

At the supposed trouting place, the lines were whipped in with vigor, and with fervor of anticipation. The brush and timber in the water were obstructions to prosperous sport. High and Pratt tottered or scrambled out on uncertain and yielding logs, and made random casts, but with no cheering results, except that Pratt was enlivened by the surprising capture of a splendid one-pounder, seemingly the solitary trout of the pool. But the chubs snuffed us as from afar, and came shortly, a collective voracity, to vex our patience, and, after viciously jerking out a few as monitory examples to the species, the anglers decamped in conspicuous dudgeon.

Awaiting the canoes and the portage of the cargoes, we lounged on the brink. My compeers yielded to the seductive biblomania and industriously yawned over their novels and lost themselves in the mazes of the plots. Unequal and not inclined to similar mental dissipation, I was content with the thoughtless idleness of smoking and watching the whiffs dissolving around me, or the ripples gently lifting and silvering on the stream. When we were again embarked and not long under way, the much-seeing Kaquotash distinguished a deer in a scarcely visible clump of bushes, and advanced the canoe more briskly thereaway. But he could get no nearer than within long rifle range, and the bullet sent from his trusty piece only served to speed the deer rushingly off into the dense timber.

We came, then, to an almost inappreciable brook weakly filtering, as it were, drop by drop, from some neighboring spring, into the river. It is only where the cold thrills of the springs are imparted by these veins of water to the main stream, that haunts of Michigami trout can be found or expected. Pratt had his eye on this tiny outlet, and was the first to cast as we rounded to. He had the luck of starting some lively rises for a time, but not the equal fortune of capturing. He brought in only three or four. Each one that he lost seemed to him lustier than the last, and, of course, his complacency became more jangled and correspondingly out of tune.

About six o'clock, on reaching a bend, a splendid sight surprised, and at the same time, hushed us into the silence of admiration and caution. Straight ahead were the stately forms of a couple of bucks, one of grand size, with a lordly foliage of antlers towering up; his consort buck, also, not meagerly branched with horns, and with them a beautiful doe. They were in full view fronting us, grouped together in mid-stream, a wondrous picture of majesty and gracefulness, worthy to be sculptured into enduring marble, as they stood. The larger buck seemed fixed in a pose of pride, as if contemplating his own massive proportions in the mirror of the stream. He and his fellow then dropped their fronts to the water, and gracefully arched them up again; threw them back erect, and tossed off the water that showered like spray, and again repeated the dip, and appeared as if about, another time, to plunge their antlers, when the big-horned buck slowly turned his head, as if first to scent any impending or possible danger.

In the meantime our Indians instinctively crouched low, like tigers for a spring, and motioned us to perfect quiet, though we already were spontaneously and breathlessly still. The forward canoe crept on stealthily and slowly, with strokes of the paddles which expert Indian woodsmen and canoeists only have the knack of making noiseless. Our canoe was silently moving in the wake of the forward one, our eyes fixed, as by a spell, we scarcely respiring, for fear a breath even would dispel the charm of the scene.

> "Ah! what a pity were it to disperse,
> Or to disturb so fair a spectacle,
> And yet a breath can do it."

It really was a scene too rare and fine to last longer than for momentary view.

Before the advance vessel could move the shooters into effective range, we were sighted and scented, and quick like thought, the group broke up; the bucks and doe and the triggers all went together, and, with head thrown back, the deer plunged and dashed, in a foam of the water, to the shore, and receded like a flash into the thick covert of bushes, "lost to sight, but to memory, dear." For a few seconds we were still under the trance, and then nearly all, simultaneously, broke out in a loud whoop of relief. Our boys, George and Paul, twitted and chaffed the forward Indians for the luckless *fiasco* of their marksmanship and strategy. Denison was sadly crest-fallen over the event.

Afterwards, in the camp, it was remarked that Denison did not, with his rueful countenance, look like the same man, to which another of the party twinklingly responded, the deer, though, *were* the same deer. David's rifle fired no better than Denison's shot-gun. The range was long, and it was no fault of either that he was forced to fire afar. Except in rounding a bend, and surprising one, it is not easy to get a dead shot at a deer. Even in a near drawing on him, and more especially when the range is distant, the greater or less oscillation and motion of the canoe is likely to waver or swerve the line of sight, and make the shooting something unsure and wild.

Kaquotash betrayed earnest meditation in his face, as if pondering how yet to show us something in the way of deer-slaying. He steered us for encamping to a high bank with dense pines overhanging, and to this particular place, because there was a known deer haunt in the vicinity. He purposed making a night hunt with the lantern to redeem himself and retrieve the mischance of the afternoon. And such was Denison's humor too. His blood was up, and his rage for deer was now inappeasable. In the kindled fervor of the two, we had a sure forecast of venison.

After the cups and platters of supper were disposed of, and the night set in, the gunners held a divan on the grass, and arranged the strategy of a dark hunt. Denison tacked the lantern on his hat so that when the slide was moved its glare would shoot out far in the abyss of darkness, like that of a light-house signal. With Dixon and Thebault to man the canoe, he vanished into the distance and the night up the river. Kaquotash and Paul footed it, through the shadows of the pines, to a neighboring pond or lakelet. High, Pratt and I, in musing meditation fancy free, the while, lay on the blankets, wistfully, and principally watching the flare of the blazes of the camp fire, or the smoke of our meerschaums wreathing visible fragrances around us. Our own voices were the only sounds that broke the dead silence of the night.

We waited not long. The report of the gun was heard, and, speedily, Denison followed it to camp, and laid before us the trophy of a slain doe. We hailed him with congratulatory pæans. Pratt was enough elated to vow, and give formal notice, that in honor of the event, he would next morning decorate himself in the gala costume of a new shirt collar. Denison quite modestly bore his blushing honors, considering that he never before shed deer's blood, and though not bearing himself with any particular air of flushing or vaunting, he was notably complacent in manner, as if, now, amends were made for his flash in the pan shortly before, and as if we were now bound to rate his gunning at its real worth. David was less fortunate. He wearily and patiently scouted the margins of the pond, and laid in wait, and noiselessly slipped the canoe from point to point, but no sign of a deer was heard or seen, and he was obliged to return with his redemptory purpose left for future achievement.

Frank's venison, when served on the breakfast log, was not a tender viand; but as it was the first of the kind, we proposed making an honest meal of it. I noticed it was not, however, until the second liberal course had gone the round of the platters, that any one ventured absolutely to affirm that the venison was rather tough. We thought it would be ungracious to Denison, and it would seemingly be to misprize the excellence of the meat and detract from the lustre of his achievement for us to be critical about the cohesive quality of the flesh. So we smacked our lips on it as a delicacy and declared the repast a feast.

## CHAPTER XI.

VOCATION OF ARMS AND REVOLVER SHOOTING — TRYING FOR TROUT—DRIFT-PILE—TROUT DINNER—A PORCUPINE AND PORCUPINES — MARBLE — A CARNIVAL OF MINKS — PARTRIDGES — FLOPPERS — A WINDFALL — UPPER MICHIGAMI FALLS — MOISTURE — LITERATURE.

WE recognized Denison's vocation as one of arms. His revolver and gun and ammunition-box were his playthings. He apparently thought the best service of his cold steel was its being kept hot by use. Loading and firing were his favorite diversions. Popping gun or pistol was a necessity, and if no living thing offered itself to his marksmanship, a bump or spot on a tree served for target practice. A chunk was floating past, and he challenged me to revolver practice with him. I pulled away at the chunk. I claimed that the ball had perforated its centre, as there was no splash of the water. But he and the others, as his corroborative witnesses, with one voice, declared I had missed even the river and shot into the sandbank beyond. As the verdict was against me I was at least silenced, if not satisfied.

When we were again on the way, Pratt discovered a brooklet putting in. In the cool water of its confluence with the river, he knew there were the conditions of a resort for trout. So the canoes were paddled to the mouth of the brook and halted. He switched in his fly, and whipped a nest of trout into most animated commotion for a brief while. He took in a few of the leapers; but just at once the whole shoal of trout must have abruptly emigrated, in a panic, to safer parts, for not another rise was to be had.

No sooner had we swung off and were under way, than David's eye discerned a deer ahead; but, though cautiously dropping the canoe toward it, the deer took the alarm and went flying, so the shot aimed at it whizzed a harmless errand. So, too, after a mile of further paddling, we came within view of a buck nibbling his morning herbage. He stopped not on the order of leaving his unfinished feeding, and Denison's buckshot effected nothing but to speed him to a masterly retreat into the woods.

We came to a gorge of drift-wood, which looked like the *debris* of a forest chaotically jammed fast; it was about a quarter of a mile of piled-up heaps and jaggedness, so solidly wedged and massed that the floods could not move it. We trailed over the carry, and the boys shouldered the canoes and cargoes around. Below this, a handsome, but incautious doe, stepped into the brink to ford the river. She caught sight of us in time, and as our appearance was not at all pleasing to her, quicker than a whirligig, she turned tail on us and went a fast vanishing form of white.

Under the verdure of arching firs and cedars, the dinner was served. There was a carpeting of faded brown layers of fallen twigs, as soft to the footfall, as a vesture of sponge or a velvet of nature's own weaving. The ground was clear of bushes and thicket. The spread of our *cuisine* was not various, but it was, to us, eminently sufficient, as much so as if it had been prepared according to Soyer, or, as if it were an inspiration of Brillat-Savarin. We needed none of the sauces or condiments of gastronomic art to sharpen appetite, or to lend to eating a zest, and to tea-drinking a flavor unknown to *gourmets* and pampered epicures. The catching of a trout or plumping of a buck, when one, himself, brings in the fins or the horns, or is a witness to the taking off, greatly enhances the relish of the fish or the flesh on the dish.

The Roman table connoiseurs were wont to have the intended fishes of their dinners brought living before them, just on the eve of their being put to pot, that the eaters might, in the courses quickly following, have the sense of freshness to tickle their piscivorous appetites. The stoic Seneca, a sturdy moralist, has severely noted and censured this daintiness of the prandial epicures. Whoever has seen the water dripping from the trout as they are taken, then seen them prepared for the pan, touched by the fire into a rich browny crisp, and served at table, all nearly as an entire and inseparable process, knows the difference in lusciousness, flavor and delicacy between the trout of a dinner he has eaten at Chicago, and the trout of a dinner *al fresco* on the brink of their native Michigami. Such trout meals on the river, are something of the luxurious, to be remembered.

On the afternoon down way we stopped to cast at the mouth of a stream, but a few rises seemed to exhaust the local sport. All along the water where there were sloughs, grass patches or swamps, fresh deer tracks were innumerably imprinted. At the mouth of Fence river, which sluggishly came in, nearly hidden in a luxuriance of grass, the sands at the margin were trampled into mire by the countless hoofs of the herds that frequent there. A couple of porcupines were airing themselves on a driftwood log, and immovably stared us in the face. But Denison with his unerring revolver and at short range went by, and they will fret their lives nevermore. The charges scattered many of their quills on the water.

On starting out next morning, Denison and I took the forward canoe. At a brook that ran in over a rocky bed, the other canoe was held up and lagged for trouting. We moved on ahead, and saw another phenomenally large porcupine snuffing the open morning air, and his prickles glistening in the sun. We bore down on him at close quarters. I offered him the compliments of a revolver salute, and Denison tendered him the liberal civilities of three shots. These amenities were lost on him. With his quills fretfully bristling out, he scrambled off, unharmed, up the log to his retreat.

Further on, David ran us in at a white marble ledge on the bank. He landed himself and knocked off specimen fragments for us. He told us that off from the river, there was a hill of fine white marble. Possibly, some day, blocks quarried there may be reared into palaces or sculptured into monumental effigies. But as we had no thought of erecting palatial edifices in the metropolis, Chicago, and still less of providing for ourselves grave-yard shafts in the necropolis, Graceland or Oakwood, David's samples and information therefore failed to warm us into a mineralogical fervor.

But though this geological formation was of no interest to us, a zoological display which we witnessed was a jocund, though an exceedingly fleeting, entertainment. It was a hilarious rabble of minks, frisking and capering festively on the sand, squealing a merry chorus, and in the very heighth of frolic as we, unbidden and unwelcome strangers, hove around a bend into the midst of the revel. Denison was as much surprised as the minks were, and though their stampede was a marvel of dispersive celerity, he was quick enough on trigger to make one panic-stricken mink bite the sand. Kaquotash went ashore and appropriated the carcass. He said its pelt was just what he wanted for a tobacco pouch. Nor was this the only animal trophy of Denison. There was a brace of partridges sanding their craws. After he fired into one of them, there was very little that was sandy, but a good deal that was leaden, in the demised partridge's maw. But broiled partridge enriched our next bill of fare.

We startled a flock of "sawbills" or "floppers." They are fish-eating ducks, but not themselves eatable of sportsmen. David apprised us that this family of quackers is a numerous aquatic nuisance on the Michigami. They partly run and partly fly along the stream, and, with their wings and webs flapping the water, and harshly quacking as they go, make a boisterous flight that can be heard at a distance. They always keep in the van of the navigator, and when out of harm's way, settle down in the water until the canoe again nearing, they scamper in another rout. The Indians predicted that this our introduction was likely to prelude a frequent, but rather distant acquaintance with the sawbills, as they would surely forerun us far down the river.

A pair of porcupines in the top branches of two neighboring trees, looking like bunches of mistletoe, fired Denison's ambition to fusilade them with his revolver. David's far-seeing eye, which took in, and always before any of our eyes had a sight, everything notable, espied a mink frantically tearing through the bushes, to its retreat. Its agility in making the run was such that Denison could only fire an equivocal shot, which harmed neither hide nor hair of the noxious creature.

We passed a windfall, where a tornado had swept, like a besom of destruction, through the forest, and left towering pines, firs and cedars prostrate in chaotic heaps and confusion, to mark its terrific devastation. To realize the utter and fearful havoc of a whirlwind in its career of fury and madness, one needs only see its swath and pathway of wreck and ravage in a Michigan pinery.

We reached the portage to Michigami falls about one o'clock. Denison and myself, with our Indians, managed, by vigorous footing, to make the lower end of the trail just as the heavy clouds, which we had seen following darklingly over the back-ground, spread over us, and burst into drenching torrents of rain. The shelter-tent afforded some protection.

Our messmates and suite who had but just reached the upper end of the carry in the midst of the shower, fared less fortunately. The turned-up canoe, under which they tried to compress themselves, was but a mockery of shelter against the merciless drench. In the meantime, spite of the rain, shortly moderating, the natives were able to start a fire. The blazes of the roaring heap were cheering warmth and glowing welcome to High and Pratt, when, soaked and dripping, they stalked into camp. None the less did we pleasantly greet their coming in because of the splendid mess of trout which they had picked up on the way, in the rear. They had come upon a family of deer, a buck, doe and fawn, swimming the river, but, as they were without the necessary deadly weapon, they had no means of creating a disturbance or a loss in the group, and the fortunate trio passed scathless on its way, admirable as a vision, but unavailing as venison.

These upper falls are not a very grand and wild freak of nature, in the way of a cascade; there is no precipitous, sheer deadfall of water over an edge or precipice, but the river compresses its volume into a narrow space between a point of rocks on one side and a rocky wall on the other, the water pitching in terraces, down an incline; the cliff rears straight aloft, probably a hundred or more feet, and is heavily garnished with small stunted cedars and pines; there is also nothing striking in the scenery. Some of the party thought the basin promising for trout, and, after the clouds cleared away, paced along the margin from point to point, and dropped in their lines with the persistence of cheering hope, and then skimmed around in the canoe, from one and another current or eddy; but the only signs or responses to the fly were from the aggravating chubs. The trout there, if any, were too wary for the party.

No useless time, however, was lost in tentative casting. It was our fate to lie idly by the rest of the day, with wet goods to hang over the fire, to dry the tents and patch the leaks in the birchen fleet. In the later monotony of the afternoon, the literary fever rather vehemently struck us. In the brilliant flashes of silence, and while the genial warmth of the fiery log heaps soothed us, each one yielded to the sorcery of the book. Denison was absorbed in the "American Senator," possibly dreaming or hoping to be one. Pratt took a shine to "Joshua Haggard's Daughter." High devoted his intellect to "Heaps of Money." I sharpened my appetite for the coming supper of trout, by reading of trout in honest Walton's pages. While we were so occupied, the shadows stole on and deepened into night.

# CHAPTER XII.

SCARECROW DUCKS—CAMPING PLACE—EASE, REST, ISOLATION—A RAVEN—THE RIVER—LAKE MARY—NATURAL PARK CAMP—IN CAMP—PAINT RIVER—RED ROOSTER AND SQUAW—DERELICT CANOE—THE FOUNDLING—HARD NAVIGATION—PAINT FALLS—A MOUSE STORY.

AFTER the vesper meal of trout, the sawbill plague was a prominent theme of indignant confabulation. The pernicious water-tramps had during the day verified Kaquotash's ill report of them, in their appearance, from time to time, at the front of us. On our nearing them the flock would start up and off, keeping to the water, winnowing it as they moved on, boisterously splashing and harshly squawking, so as to make them a moving van of scarecrows to all the game in the woods. When the flock preceded us to the falls, it kept on in the current and swept along with the whirl of the torrent, and reappeared resilient out of the vortex below, as so many corks bobbing up from a forced submersion.

Our camp was so well conditioned by night, when we were rested and dried, that we enjoyed in it the combined pleasures—ease, comfort and content. The blazing trunks of pines equally brightened and warmed us ; the rumble of the falling waters and the lulling murmur of the stream in our front made soothing music for the senses; the light of the swinging lamp enlivened the interior of the tent. We gossiped into late hours, and with good cheer of mirth and laughter—for there is no place like a forest camp-mess for stories and fun—we smoothed the way to slumber, that was refreshing and sweet.

The complete repose of mind, with no thought of shop and with but little of the world or of the war in Europe, of the news and life of the day at home even, was the charm and blissfulness of our scenes and pastimes in the far-off unpeopled wilderness. Here were none of the pervading agencies of civilization, business and industry, with their cares and importunities—elsewhere ever ceaseless—to perturb our mental isolation and quiet. No railway and its rushing train; no telegraph stretching as mystic chords to bear us thrills of message from our homes; no daily journal to mirror us a life other than our own; no presences to link us to the world beyond our immediate horizon. It was this mental repose that made our hemlock couches as soft as beds of roses and sleep so deep and refreshing. It was this that made every encampment seem a happy Arcadia of peace and content.

We vanished from the dashing of the Michigami Falls. The clouds were threatening, and their pluvial omens were soon realities of showering. The drops streaked down the glaze of the ponchos in harmless watery films or veins. A good many puffs of foam, like great white sponges, floated from the falls. The rain pattered the stream into broadcast tiny bubbles. A raven winged a high flight over our heads, and flew shyly and croaked spitefully at us, as if he were averse to human society, and was, evidently, not in his nature akin to the friendly raven that fed the holy prophet with bread.

Three miles from the start David espied a far-off deer in the brush, and saluted it with a rifle-ball, which clipped the twigs close by, and started it snorting with fright into the safe asylum of the woods. The crack of the gun sounded an alarum to our evil genii, the floppers, which scooped along the water and clamorously squawked down the stream.

The river swelled into wider bounds as we proceeded, with fewer rapids and shallows, but bordered with a vivid density of forest and uniformity of wildness. We were in a silent domain of all unsubdued nature. The sprays of the pines moved neither with the gentle sway or tremor of a breeze or with the quiver of a bird. The scenery appeared brooding in a calm as still as the landscape of a picture, but with an exuberance of richness which no pencil of art, but only the touch of nature, could produce.

At noon, we landed at the portage to Lake Mary. It was a scarcely visible entrance to a labyrinth of bushes and woods, the pathway of which was tortuous and barely traceable, and beset, throughout, with undergrowths that had to be bent or brushed aside, and made our footsteps tardy and weary. When we emerged from the density and touched the edge of the lake, the little sheet shone in the radiance of the sun like a glittering mirror in a leafy setting of emerald. The azure of the sky and the snowy clouds were reflected in its pure depths, an imaged heaven, each seeming the other, the sky the water and the water the sky, without a wayward zephyr rippling it with a breath to wrinkle or disturb the picture. While the boys were lugging over the canoe and the stowage, we had full time, reclining on the grassy slope, to restfully muse and enjoy the summer glories blended in the scene.

The water was crystally clear. We thought it must be stocked with fish. When the canoes were in motion, trolling lines were put out, but uselessly. The lake curved, and was not wholly seen in a first view. Around the bend, the panorama of lake and shores spread out more charmingly, though the sheet was not a large one. The stillness of the whole scene was impressive. Little of life was heard or seen. A solitary loon, moaning its plaintive notes, lamentable as a sepulchral wail, was the only sound or sign of living thing on its silent expanse.

We made the further end of the lake, about a mile, at a knoll swelling gently up from the little cove or nook in which the canoes were landed. The undergrowth had at some period doubtless been burned out, and the forest thinned by fire, yet with enough scattering green-flourishing pines and firs left by the destroying scourge for shade, and to make the several acres of rolling surface a handsome, natural park. On the summit of the lawn, velvet with carpeting green, the tents were ultimately placed for the day. A rain, with repeated accessories of thunder and lightning ripping closely over us, copiously outpoured, for a time, and streamed down the canvas roofing.

Most of the time during the afternoon we were housed in for shelter, as the dropping of the clouds was nearly constant. Ourselves snug and dry within, the cheap novels, at such a time resources of some utility, served to relieve the situation of much of its dreariness, and to make the party unconcerned about the action of the elements. The Indians, in their tented lair, comforted themselves with cards and tobacco. After night set in and the repast was finished, and the clouds had dispersed, the camp-fire cheerily lapped the great pine heap in jets and tongues of flame and we squatted around it.

Our spirits brightened in the glow of the genial blazes, and the crackling of the flames was out-noised by the lively chatter of much-speaking lips. The forms of the smoke, fantastically rising and vanishing like spectral shadows into the night above, were not lighter and more varying than our wantoning fancies. Memories of other woodland scenes, or of wanderings of other days, were recalled. We heard Denison's story of his mountain travel in the West, of his ascent of Pike's Peak, and of the more perilous climb of Long's peak, as well. Hours were thus passed, near unto the witching time of night, and were made the pleasanter by those friendly and ready servitors of all the hours of some of us—the meerschaum pipes. The night's camp-fire lighted the shrine of memory with a blazonry of recollections delightful and enduring, and, for the time, at least, paled the memories of the firelights on the hearthstones at home.

The waking in the morning was to a rat-tat of rain pattering on the tent. The showering, however, gradually softened into a mist, and finally that vanished, though the clouds still hovered in the sky, portending other coming rain. But neither such prognostics of ill-weather nor the beauty of the landscape there could delay us from a quickstep advance towards attractive regions beyond.

It is a two mile portage to the Paint river. To aid the Indians, each of us swung some parcel of his own outfit over his shoulder or gripped it in his hands, and tottered burdensomely along the tortuous footway. Bearing these fardels was, with some of us at least, to grunt and sweat under a weary load, very unlike the burdens we were accustomed to carry. Denison, however, rather plumed himself on having achieved a prodigy in the instance of his transportation. To throw our portable capacities in the shade and vaunt his own, he troubled himself to weigh in the fish scales, one by one, the separate parcels of his load. The total pounds avoirdupois were fifty-seven. As the Indians made light of packs more than double that weight, he thought he would scarcely hoist flying colors, or very particularly allude to the sinews of Hercules or the shoulders of Atlas.

By noon the carrying was finished. The trail led to a high bank or knob of a hill, and had a cleared space for former camping. It overlooked a broad, smooth reach of the Paint river, skirted with borders of unbroken forest. At the foot of the hill, a little brook, hidden under interlacing branches, and cold with the chill of its supplying or parent springs, ran into the stream. Doubtless it was a very covert for shoals of trout. High and Denison must have had an insight of this, for they set out with rods and baskets, to find some accessible silent nook or recess free enough of limbs and brush wherein to cast the fly. Wherever they pushed on they found the little stream impenetrably guarded and hedged against the art and patience of all anglers, by the density of defensive overgrowth and undergrowth.

We had dinner there. Just while we were taking the last morsels of our meal, a canoe hove into port with a freight of three—a Chippewa gentleman, barefoot, and two squaws of the same aboriginality, apparently matron and maid. The ladies timidly looked at us, and quietly maintained their broad, squat and bundle-like position in the canoe, seeming to imply that as "white men are mighty uncertain," they would prefer to keep their distance. So they remained and rode at anchor.

Red Rooster, or whatever his name was, knowing some of our Indians, and, possibly sniffing in his sensitive nostrils the disseminating aroma of diet, intrepidly climbed or hoisted himself up the hill to camp, and began to pow-wow the natives of the retinue. Cordial relations were soon established, and the Menominee or Chippewa vernacular was the medium of their voluble civilities. One word of it, "*now-o-kah,*" or an expression very like that, seemed to reach a most tender spot in Red Rooster's capacious diaphragm. We took it to be the Menominee phrase for pot-luck or grub, and the Chippewa evidently considered himself an invited guest.

He evinced a most accommodating alacrity at taking a chair, by straddling a log, at the table, which was a packing-box upside down. He was not taking his dinner in courses, but made a promiscuous onset on all the dishes. He was not mealy-mouthed in familiarizing himself with the potatoes. He was not at all prejudiced against the Japan tea. A second supply of it seemed beatifying. That Indians, as some speculators theorize, are not descendants of the lost tribes of Israel, the havoc he made in the pork side-dish was sufficient proof. His proclivity for the cooked hog would silence a suspicion of the remotest kinship or affinity to the Jews. In fact, all our cooking was precisely to his taste. He showed what he could do when he had a chance at high living like ours.

If not told the dining guest was a Chippewa, we might have believed him a Gros Ventre. The greedy savage lost his gallantry in his glut, for never a morsel did he bear to the crone and maid in the canoe, though we offered for them the hospitality of the *cuisine.* They knew our tea only by its vapors, and our pork by its odor. It was all a Barmecide feast to them.

Red Rooster and the ladies were going in our direction, foraging for game. So, when we embarked, he and they embarked and consorted with us. He and our men poled the canoes side by side, and kept up fluent guttural clack between the pushes. The women shared liberally in the palaver, and evinced the civilized sex's fluency of speech. Over in the bushes, David espied a half-concealed birch-bark canoe, dry-docked in a bower of leaves. He ran in, and landed himself to inspect the treasure trove, determined, if it were a prize, to condemn and appropriate it by Indian law, as derelict.

David and Paul hauled the canoe out of her cunning embosomment of leaves, and submitted her to close inspection. They set to work at repairing her by smirching the cracks and seams in her birchen sheathing with a glaze of resin and pitch.

The Indian ladies stepped ashore to lend hands to David in the process. It was nothing to them to step out in the wet. Their kips and Balbriggan hose, if such effeminate trifles they had, were away in their far-off wigwam domicile. They waded about in the water like Naiades, and daubed on the streaks of pitch like experts.

I had an interview with one of the female dabsters, who was melting resin by puffing flame on it from a burning chunk. I said: "Please let me have your fire to light a cigar," in my language. She passed it to me with a mellifluous "Ugh," in her language. The interview was thus short, but mutually agreeable and suave.

Finally, when the canoe was thought water-tight, it was launched into its native element. We named it the Foundling, to give its history in the name. David and myself, after shifting part of the load to the Tom King, went on in the new shallop. Denison and Paul paddled their own canoe. The Dickey, with High and Thebault, had stolen away a long advance march on us. A couple of miles further we parted with our Chippewa consort, which turned off in a branch around an island, on an exploration for muskrat, mink and deer. David presented the vermilion dames, who had helped him patch the Foundling, with a perfumed cake of Babbitt's soap.

We found the Paint, on but short acquaintance, to be a hard stream up which to run our prow. It is broad, shallow and rapid, and but for the Sunday rain, which drained into it and overlaid its shoals as well as speeded its currents, we must have fought our way, light-laden as was our craft, inch by inch. Even as it was, in many places advance was a tedious scuffle, and frequently David was forced to wade and drag the pinnace by the nose. Once, too, I was obliged to take to water, to lighten the canoe over shallows that were merely a ragged and threadbare cover of stream.

We reached the Paint Falls, though but seven or eight miles from our embarkation point on this river, just in time to catch the last roseate flushes of sunset on the water, crimsoning it as if a stream of blood had run red into it from the carnage of a battle-field, a glory of color worthy of a Claude to paint. The falls are a broad curving break, with a low rock formation, large boulders upheaving their bold fronts in places, the water parting around them in foaming currents, so that, on the approach from below, the cascade looked like slopes of ground, streaked and patched with drifts of snow.

The camp was at the further end of the carry around the falls. A space for the tents had to be cleared of bushes and branches, which rapidly fell before the strokes of Thebault's axe. Though a huge drift-pile was near by, a gorge of pines of many freshets, it was difficult to get wood for warming and cooking. There had been no campers here before us this year. We were the pioneers of the season. Pratt and High found places to drop their flies, and were skilled enough to befool a mess of fifteen glistening trout from the pools, which were served in their sweetest freshness and flavor on the supper platters.

The ill-omened gang of Michigami sawbills, or some of their detestable kind, had forerun us here. They disturbed the serenity of Denison's temper, and, after a bit of strategy for a good position, he fired a hail of shot into the flock, and, by a good fortune which is rare in the case of this wary duck, one of them was killed. When it was brought in by the canoe, and laid at his feet, Frank exulted over the dead fowl. It was the proudest moment of his life, and so forth. He took a Falstaff attitude, "there lies Percy for you!" He has such an antipathy against this species of the duck, that if he could, by one murderous explosion, blow the whole flock of these disturbing nomads into annihilation, he would ask no other laurel, and would return home without again trying to strike a trout or shoot a deer.

From our camping fire, at night, the flames threw up a ruddy glare which tinged the massive foliage of the great pines into illuminated drapery of fantastic shapes. In the genial radiance, we brightened, and the dark solitudes and depths of the wood echoed the noise and laughter of the camp. Denison related us the thrilling story of a mouse prodigy. His office was infested with mice, which nibbled and chewed his chancery files, and they were too wary for the cheap device of a mouse-trap. He charged a shot-gun with small shot, and laid for the petty spoilers. One of them crept out slyly, just in the nick of time to draw his shower of leaden mustard seed. He fired away at it, but the mouse slunk back to its retreat, as he supposed with a whole skin. Next day, in turning over the papers, he found the mouse laid out, defunct.

The odd and curious part of Denison's story was that the mouse had practiced a bit of surgery on itself by having plugged a shot-wound in its side with a wad of paper to stanch hemorrhage! On this relation Pratt simply ejaculated, "Well, I declare!" High said he begged to consider the story as bordering on the marvelous. I added, "Frank, your affidavit on that." He declared his readiness to swear to it, and as a Master in Chancery would administer the oath himself. High gave his professional opinion that an oath administered before himself, as Master in Chancery, by himself to himself, was a legal nullity, and he thought a solecism, and he believed no precedent could be found in the books to warrant such practice, and, in fact, such an oath, in the language of the law of Wouter Van Twiller's time, was *nix noot*. As Denison was too scrupulous to prostitute the important functions of a Chancery Master, or to trifle with the solemn formalities of the law, the *jurat* was dispensed with, and each one was left to his own meditations on the mouse.

# CHAPTER XIII.

THE FOUNDLING ABANDONED—RARITY OF BIRDS—MORE SAW-BILLS—A PORTAGE—A PORCUPINE—TROUT RIVER CAMP—A SNAKE INCIDENT—A BEAR INCIDENT TOO—TROUT RIVER—PILLARS OF HERCULES—FLATS AND SHALLOWS—DIFFICULT NAVIGATION—BEAVER DAM—AN EAGLE—LAKE CHICAGON——CHRISTENING OF LAKE MINNIE.

THE current of the Paint was so stiff that two men were required to run the canoes. We could not make such a distribution of muscular power as was necessary, if we took the waif canoe further on. So we left the Foundling, high and dry in the woods, for some succeeding party to pick up and appropriate.

The river above the falls was broader, shallower, and more rapid than below. At many places, the navigators waded and dragged the birches along, and at one point, all of us stepped out and wetted our shins and trousers in the shallow. The party in the Dickey was in the lead. We had the tantalizing but useless privilege of seeing three deer wading over, on their southward emigration way, without any means of making anything but a distant acquaintance of them, for want of guns.

Denison, in our boat, had a chance shot at an overflying straggling flopper, and exultingly slaughtered the flagitious duck, and not long after caught sight, in the far-off perspective, of a lively moving buck in a dissolving view. Our way was through a monotony of dense foliage of vivid green, a very huge wall, or precipice-like mass of verdure, seemingly planted on the water itself, so few and scant were the patches of naked shore, and so meagre were the strips of sand on the edge of the stream.

Beyond the water front, all was solitary and untrodden wilderness. We remarked everywhere, thus far, the exceeding rarity of bird-life in these immensities of woods. Few are the " wood-notes wild " of forest songsters. The twigs and branches but seldom bend or sway with the pressure of plumages. The silence of the forest is solemn and death-like. At this season, even the water-fowl are not numerous. A kingfisher sometimes swooped down from a hanging branch, to make a scoop of small fry, or, scared by us, darted from his perch of observation, with an angry scream, to a limb further away. Ducks were yet unseasonable—that is, those that a sportsman would covet for his game-bag. The pestilent congregation of floppers which heralded our advance, or their congeners, was not wanting. It was rather early, too, for the herds of migrating deer.

We had so slowly worked a way up, that it was noon before we touched our landing-place. It was a portage of a half mile. It was the usual trail of roughness and narrowness, of masses of foliage and net-work of bushes. On the way, we passed wild cherry trees. Of their red fruitage the bears are particularly greedy. It was not strange, then, that unmistakable bear tracks imprinted the path, and that there were other signs of recent ursine presence and cherry-tree spoliation. Very naturally, therefore, an emergency of bear could not be thought improbable, and so a look-out was kept, and the armor of defense, in the hands of Denison, was kept in a state of preparation for instant action; that is to say, the gun to shower buck-shot and the somewhat damaged belt-knife to do the jabbing and ripping business.

But in our progress of armed caution no beast more savage or perilous than a porcupine was encountered, and that one was taking a survey of the country, doubtless, from the topmost limb of a lofty pine. Denison had renewed porcupine entertainment on this occasion, and in the contest for life which ensued Denison prevailed, and the porcupine dropped suddenly from his lofty perch, in obedience to the inflexible law of survival of the fittest. We came to an inexpressibly paltry and dismal lakelet, or really pond, of dead water. It had at a distance a sickly greenish hue, like that of the scurf of a frog-pond. But this semblance of green slime was, in fact, caused by the countless water-lilies whose leaves were spread flat, as if drooped and prostrated by some vegetable epidemic blight, and overlapped thickly like fish scales. We crossed this mess of water and lily pads. In the sand where we landed fresh imprints betokened recent presence of deer.

The portage thence to Trout river was a mile and a half of the usual multitudinous impediments of the trail. Though we should reach the end and the night together, we at once set out on the wearisome tramp. To afford us speedier and easier carrying, the canoes were beached on the shore, to be taken over in the morning. The place for encampment was a dreary, low, swampy, malarious pine-flat, more uninviting and deepened into unpleasantness, from the gloomy shadows of the twilight. The atmosphere was moist and dank. It was a geographical necessity—a Hobson's choice, a clear case of willy-nilly—that obliged us to content ourselves with that as our place of nocturnal sojourn. Trout river was a few rods off. In the last leaden somberness of the day, we could discern a cheerless outlook of a crooked, narrow, sluggish channel of open stream, in a meadow or broad margin of ooze, bottomless mud, and water lilies, where a sand-hill crane would mire in the slime or get tangled in the thick-set plant of reeds and grasses.

How we were, in the morning, to tide canoes, cargoes, and ourselves, over the marshy and nasty morass, to the free water, was a quandary of speculation. The dilemma had to be turned over, for solution, to the engineering resources of the Indians. We had trust in David's wood-craft experience. He looked the spirit of Virgil's hero, *aut inveniam viam aut faciam*, and we were confident he would find a way, or make a way. It was impossible, from the end of the trail, for him to get directly to the river for even enough water for supper purposes. Access was gained by a long oblique of route to the water, but after much experimental patience and exploration. He told us that only by a liberal swing of the ax, in some places, and corduroying or pontooning the slumps with branches at others, a way of extrication to the river was possible.

Spite, however, of adverse surroundings, and first impressions, the blazes of the camp fire tipped the shadowing trees with ruddy tinges, and sent up fire-flies of sparks dotting the whirls of smoke, and the camp was robed in a livery of light. By the time the supper platters were set before us, after unusual delay in the preparation, our appetites were sharpened to unwonted fineness of edge, and the supper's eating was something voracious. The moral effects of the repast, as well as the enlivening transformation scenes wrought around us by the brilliant flames of pine, much elevated and cheered the tone of the party. We settled ourselves to the conviction that we were not far from being happy, and could accept the situation in much good humor and with exceeding grace. We fell into a lively babble of tongues, little less than exhilarating.

David interested us with many of his forest reminiscences and, like another Scheherezade, became a narrator of Indian Night's Entertainments. One of these night entertainments made a sensation. It was peculiarly topical and *apropos* in its bearing; it was an incident of a former camping party at this very spot. While the campers were wrapped in the lulling embrace of Morpheus, three large snakes crawled into the tent; one of these wriggled over the uncovered shin of one of the sleepers, and, as if an elongated icicle were drawn over the tibia, with such frigid effect as to bring him to his immediate senses. The impromptu scene of midnight panic and confusion that followed, was indescribable. This reptilian reminiscence had a bad effect on us, and chilled our fervency of spirit, and induced crawling sensations in each particular spine of the party.

"Be there bears i' th' town?—they are very ill-favored, rough things." Master Slender's inquiry and his zoological hint would have been in order in our camp. Kaquotash's tale of serpents put us in a kind of cold shiver that the blankets could not entirely warm away. To have been surprised in our sleeping, by a serpent creeping in the tent and coiling in one of the manly bosoms there, might not now have appeared supernatural or quite out of the course of the fitness of things in a Trout river swamp. But the fate of being hugged to the bosom of an unceremonious black bear! It is not easy to say how nearly some of us came to realizing such an unexpected embrace. In fact, in "the dead vast and middle of the night," and out of the wilderness, while we were sunk in the depth of sleep, a veritable bear did loom into appearance and stalk around the camp, crackling the dry brush, stirring the bushes and leaving his paws imprinted in the mud. He ranged closely enough to us to prove that he meant no good and was on no peaceful errand. He was smelling about for our provision stores, doubtless, with a keen snout and watering mouth, and, it may be, with designs on the occupants of the tent as well as on the commissariat.

High sometimes sleeps with one eye open, or was at least, on half ocular watch for swamp-snakes at the time, and knew what was afoot. He sounded a tocsin of alarm. Denison awoke rather confused, and probably having just been dreaming himself a Laocoon in the coil of the serpents, or of wrestling in the compressive grip of a full-grown nightmare, and wishing to have his grapple out with the incubus or the snakes, was rather slow in coming to the front, but on realizing the situation, reached about for his trusty field-piece, and then remembered it was unloaded, after all. He requested his bed-fellow, Pratt, to turn him over his caisson, and for once it was out of the way, and not readily found. Pratt was probably somnambulistic, and not conceiving the demand, fumbled around, and, as the first thing he could lay his hands on, clutched one of High's long-legged boots. The point of Denison's savage knife was left at camp Mary sticking in a tree in which it was broken off while being pitched at a mark. For instant use, there were only the angling rods to punch out the enemy's eyes. I tried to muster enough intrepidity for the pinch from confidence in the terrifying effects of my guinea-hen hat which would make it a shield of safety against any ordinary carniverous beast. Our defensive means, therefore, were uncertain.

The pickle we were in was a pretty one; but, fortunately, our Indian allies were wide-awake, to save our figurative and our actual bacon. David was a veteran of the woods, and was as quick to hear a bear in the night as he was to sight a deer in sunlight. He had emerged from his snoring, and tip-toed out of the tent with his weapon in hand, and peered through the darkness, waiting a certain aim on the bear's closer approach. The Kaquotashes are not strangers in those parts, and the bears well know there is no foolishness about one of them when he has his rifle handy. This particular bruin seasonably took the hint and sneaked off with a lively trot into the depths of the further darkness, leaving our sustenance untouched and with but a faint sniff of the flesh-pots for his pains.

In the morning, Pratt somewhat gave himself up to mild chagrin. He thought it an ill-chance that he had not been more broad awake, so that he might have met the opportunities of the occasion by having gone and contended with the bear. Had he taken in the situation in time, doubtless, he would have stalked out, as Hamlet once appeared, with his doublet, and so-forth, all unbraced, for the enterprise, with stomach in it for the bear but that drowsiness overpowered his bloody purpose, turned it awry and lost it the name of action.

The natives hewed and cleared out a way from the camp to the water—but water thick-set with lily pads, and shallow over mud bottom, in which the canoes floundered dubiously, with decided tendencies to fixed adhesion. We finally got out of the swamp into a flowing of clear winding stream, with the scantiest depth. A beaver dam stretched a little obstruction across, and delayed the passage, while it was being knocked to pieces. A mile beyond was a tortuous chain of rapids, where the water tumbled over the stones in a bed or gutter of a width barely enough for a canoe. This passage was so densely bordered and overhung with branches, there were so many trees fallen across, and there was such a lack of navigable stream, that all the pale faces of the party took on a trifle more of paleness at the prospect of having come to a full stop. The situation seemed to be the pillars of Hercules of our route, the very *ne plus ultra*.

While we were driven to our wits' end to see a way through, the Indians were not at their wits' end, nor the journey's end, either. They prospected and pow-wowed earnestly, and presently we saw in their faces a cheery flickering that seemed to say where there is a will there must be a way. So they set to work, and, literally, made a way by picking out stones from the channel, chopping limbs, dragging out sunken brush, and lifting the canoes along, inch by inch. Our own course through the woods, by short-cut, was almost impossible. Scratches and bruises, climbing over and stooping under, and crawling on and slipping off prostrate trees, breaking down decayed timber, stumbling against roots, twisting branches aside, were some of the impediments of the tramp. Part of the way I took to the water and waded it, and, hard as it was to balance on the rounded and slippery rocks, and to keep from tumbling over, it was easier than penetrating the natural abattis, and I came out ahead at the end of the ordeal. The passage, though not more than a hundred yards direct, was a tug and toil of more than two hours.

From this passage, the river spread out into a width of shallows with soft muddy bottom, and with strips and flats of ooze and marsh along. In some places we slid through a soft mire, pushed by the setting poles, which sometimes stuck fast, and stirred up bubbles and nasty smells. While we were floundering through the quagmire, a mallard duck was reckless enough to fly and quack overhead, within reach of a charge from Denison, which dropped it near by in an inaccessible swash. In the struggles of its dying paroxysms, it bedaubed its glossy coloring with an unsightly stucco of mire.

The river soon lost some of its dreariness by expanding into a lake a mile and a half long and nearly as wide. The entrance to it was through a jungle of reeds and grasses, but further out, there was a clear expanse, that laid as smooth and still as the reflected azure in its depths. It is called, at least it was known to us as Lone Grave Lake. It owes its doleful name to the accident of having on its shore a solitary burial mound that commemorates some kind heart's affection or memory for the unknown dead, whose lonely remains repose there in the unending sleep. As a mortuary memento, in the way of funereal cogitation, however, the isolated tumulus visibly affected no known member of our party.

We converged into the river again, and it was again an ordeal—trying patience and straining muscle to force any passage. We made haste so slowly that the hours went on apace faster than we. The stream shriveled into narrowness and crooked into infinite sinuosities; the lily-pads and water grasses waved—a harvest of excrescence and pestering friction—before and around us. There were reaches of slime in which we stuck fast, and no one dared get out to lighten or push on the canoe for fear of sinking into inextricable adhesion; it was easy to deepen the poles in the mud, but the pulling out was a job. More than all, the pushing poles stirred up from the bottom ooze and feculence the foulest of smells, rivaling, as essence of stink, the combined fetor of skunk and assafœtida; as a nostril nuisance, Trout river in places, in its mildest effluvium, was as malodorous and unsavory as Chicago river in its hot dog-day exuberance of sewage and offal.

Not rarely, too, were the Menominees obliged to swing the axe. Here a fallen tree, with a radiation of limbs, there half-sunken brush-heaps, elsewhere a saw-like dentation of snags, bade defiance to paddle or pole, barring the way until they vanished before the strokes of the axe. The business of getting on was entirely too serious to admit of fooling with the porcupines we saw here and there. Denison, though, was always ready to pepper a flying duck and brought down several, apparently just to keep in practice his wing-shooting, of which he is justly proud. Kaquotash says that in the fall this river swarms with ducks of all varieties, and that they are plentier than the lilies.

After the gauntlet of difficulties so tediously passed through, we were brought to a stand-still by a formidable beaver-dam. But vexation gave way to admiration. It was a consummate piece of beaver engineering. It extended about seventy feet. In form it was an irregular curve with the extreme convex point in the channel, so as to turn the current into a dip on each side. The face was solidly embanked with earth, sloping smoothly and evenly from the top, while the mass of the structure was compacted of the most close contexture of logs, limbs, and sticks, very artfully interlaced and dovetailed. Its dimensions were such that it must have been the work of much time and multitudinous beavers, although, for such fish as could live and swim in the nasty stream, it was hardly worth a dam to the beavers to pen and impound them. Because it was a solid and fine specimen of animal construction, there was no help for us but to unload the shallops, lift them up and launch them over, and load them again.

On starting again, the further we went the

harder the tug and the heavier the drag. Tediously and wearisomely we plodded forward. About three o'clock we struck another beaver dam of lesser and ruder construction than the last one, but as it marked the end of our Trout river progress, we were not obliged to demolish or to surmount it. The portage to Lake Chicagon began there. We congratulated ourselves on emerging from a slough of despond, and appreciated more than ever the indomitable and tireless energy and patience of the aborigines. Our eight miles of trip here showed we were more long-coming than far-coming. We gladly landed, and a kindled and vivid log-heap fire soon clothed the over-arching cedars with wavering draperies of smoke. The kettle sang songs, and never more fragrantly did the delicate vapors of Japan tea exhilarate our senses than then, after the hungry experiences of the route.

There, too, Denison just missed the one chance, possibly, of a lifetime, of pluming himself with the rare spoil of Jove's royal bird. A majestic eagle furled his wings and perched on the branchless stem of a tree that had fallen across the stream below us, at easy range, in clear line and full sight, and calmly turned his piercing eye on every side, and upward, too, as if "gazing 'gainst the sun"— and was long enough there, in his regal pride of feather, for a pause of admiration and wonder on our part, and for our gunner to reach and poise a rifle at the splendid mark. Alackaday! it was his mischance that, with such a prize and trophy before him, the perfidious gun missed fire, and, of course, the monarch bird bounded up and soared away on outspread wings, toward the clouds. How we all, too, would have plumed ourselves with a quill from that eagle's pinions!

From there commenced the portage to Lake Chicagon. It was short and easy. The path was free and open. It was through a thick cedar grove. The layers of decayed and fallen twigs, yielding softly to the footsteps, were an outspread, nature-woven brussels, of rude, sober and primitive pattern, fitting ground for midnight revels of the fairies under the moon. This carry led us up to the Trout river again, just above another beaver dam. This was the largest of those constructions yet seen, compacted and interwrought of trunks of considerable trees, gnawed or cut off by saws of beaver teeth and tugged and floated into place.

From there, the ascent to the lake, whence the river issues, was about ten minutes of paddle-strokes, and its course was through a wide marshy flat of reeds, lilies and grasses. In places, the river was almost hidden or lost in the thickness of the water-growths. The passage of the canoes, parting and bending down the serried ranks of lilies and reeds, left a track behind like and as marked as a path trodden in a grain field. Near the edge of the lake, a deer was solitarily munching, but it vanished too rapidly for any gunnery of ours to put it in jeopardy.

Once out of the river, we saw spreading before us a most lovely expanse of water. It was of oblong form, and its shore outlines were indented with many small bays and a few bold promontories jutted out, and in the further sweep from us, two or three islands loomed up, seemingly mere solid masses of deep green color. It was about four miles long and half as many miles in width. The water was transparently clear and cool, and of much depth. Mackinaw trout and white fish are said to abound in its deep and pure recesses. We had no token, though, of Chicagon piscatory life. Lines were trolled, but the conjectural or reported Mackinaws did not happen, just at the time, to be in either a hungry or spooney mood, and showed no love for the glittering spoons that wavered below, so nothing was drawn in—excepting the lines.

David boldly set the course of the canoe, in which were High and myself, straight across the lake. Our frail atomy of a vessel in that pathway over was only safe as long as it was windless and the water was smooth. A boreal fluster, far short of a typhoon, or a nor'easter, even a moderate impromptu squall, would surely have swamped and foundered the canoe, and probably have consigned the crew to the Davy Jones' locker of Lake Chicagon. Our weather-wise navigator trusted to his Indian instincts as to blows or a cats-paw, or any sudden windiness, and High and I, wishing to *coup d'œil* the charming scene from a central point of view or commanding line of direction, preferred the diametrical bearing. Pratt and Denison, with an eye to a chance use of powder, navigated coastwise, hugging closely to the shore.

Of course, the elements were favorable. The sky was cloudless. The lake was as placid as if it had never tossed to the fury of a tempest; its face was as calm as though it were incapable of ever wrinkling in anger at the buffeting of a boisterous wind. The scene was really lifeless enough to be termed a dead calm. The only signs of any life were the occasional loons, some winging in the air, and some floating on the lake, and moaningly chanting. The edges of the lake lap the very roots and branches of the forest that girds it. This is said to be an effect of back-water raised into the trees by the beaver dam in Trout river. We touched the extreme end of the lake towards evening, and in the reflection, the beautiful sheet shone like a mirror, as still, and calm, and pure, as the deep azure above it, and with

"Not a span
Of its smooth surface trembling to the tune of sun-set breezes."

We had intended camping on the border of Chicagon, though twilight had not yet begun to steal on; but wood for the fire was reported as unattainable; so we turned our backs on the enchanting lake and set out on the portage to another lake, unnamed, so far as we knew, a half mile beyond. After leaving the thick wilderness of alders that bordered the water, the trail led us to and through hard-wood timber, including a fine maple grove, and woods like those of southern Illinois, free of undergrowth and with vistas beyond. This was a relief after a monotony of pine, hemlock, firs and cedars. We trudged the footway with a certain freedom, and without intrusive twigs and branches to prick or scratch us, or fallen tree-trunks to be escaladed. The fatigue was nothing.

Near the end of the trail, glimpses of the nameless lake were caught. When we came to it, and first stood on its shore, the tinges of the red sunset served to idealize the crystal sheet, and its accessories of woods and verdure, into a very scene of faery. Its surpassing witchery touched some, at least, of the admiring party into moods of sentiment and poesy. Perhaps Denison was one of the poetized or sentimentalizing ones. Doubtless, a sweet truant fancy that wandered far, or some haunting form, rising out of a mirage of memory, visible only to him, and wrought of some dear romance of the heart, possessed or spell-bound our musing comrade. For he proposed to us that we should give the charming water a fitting name.

With an intuition of the common assent, he himself officiated as the consecrating minister in the impromptu christening, and pronounced the name. Doubtless the name was the worded theme or keynote to which all the heart's tender chords were attuned, and the name was Minnie! And all of us, in spontaneous unison and sympathy, accorded in the naming—Lake Minnie! Even to us, who have no endearing associations of name to hallow it, Lake Minnie will come to frequent recollection, for it was "like a dream of poetry—beautiful exceedingly."

# CHAPTER XIV.

FINE ENCAMPMENT—A NOCTURNAL RABBIT—ADIEU TO LAKE MINNIE—THE BRULE! THE BRULE!—PRATT THE WADER. READY FOR BUSINESS—CEDAR CAMP—THE PROSPECT—A DOG IN MINNESOTA—PILFERING MINKS—A DISTURBED REVERIE—MINKS—ASSASSINATING A MINK—SUNSET FISHING, ET CETERA.

THE camping ground on the brow of the lake was a choice one. It was an elevated and dry situation. Some of the sweetest of sleep and most grateful of resting were here; and then, too, we were almost within hail of the Brulé. During the tenting here, Pratt was wakened from very balmy repose by an apparition of some eccentric animal of the manor, which finally, to his eye, took the shape of a pronounced rabbit, which had stolen into the pavilion and was wonderingly and intrepidly hopping about, prospecting the situation. When satisfied that it was neither a chimera nor a nondescript perilous beast, but, in fact, was an actual leporine creature, Pratt thought it a favorable occasion for a nocturnal study in natural history, and indulged the saucy rabbit the full freedom of the tent unmolested, so that he might take his observations. The presumptuous puss, finding only a stubble-field of unshaved faces lying around, presently trotted out and back to its burrow.

Some of us thought, however, when told of the incident, that it was probably a hare-brained conceit, a mere phantom-rabbit or a fantastic coinage of distempered sleep, caused by the excessive pork, potatoes and fried corn-dodgers of a late supper, or one of those spectral "shapes that haunt Thought's wilderness." But Pratt vehemently repelled the phantasmagoria theory, and avouched it a veritable and categorical rabbit, indigenous to the soil of that, and not an illusion of Thought's, wilderness. He protested that he was not fooled of his own senses, and that rabbit will be an immutable article of his faith until his dying day.

We started at eight o'clock in the morning, and paddled with metaphorical flying colors, cheerily and exultingly, as if our barks were similitudes of that in Cole's Voyage of Life, which coursed buoyantly, "with Youth at the helm, and Pleasure at the prow." Every stroke of the paddle moved us so much nearer to the Brulé, and with our faces turned thitherward, we lingered not in our parting with the pure and beauteous Lake Minnie. Our footsteps were quicker, our spirits were more bounding, and the trudge over was easier and more willing than those of any previous march afoot. When we strained the sight to peer ahead, and caught glimpses of the stream through the forest, and heard the murmurs of the water, and then descended to the foot of the hill at the river brink, we could fancy something of the thrill of the Greeks, on the return from their far expedition, at the first sight of the longed-for scene, in their gladsome shout, "The sea! the sea!" So from us, there was a vociferous impromptu of "The Brulé! The Brulé!"

While the Indians were on the portage with the canoes and stores, we had leisure for overhauling the tackle, as well as for musing, lounging, smoking and resting. But such was the ardor of Pratt's piscatorial impetuosity, an apparent emotional insanity, to forestall the sport, that though the river at that point offers no tempting prospects for fishing, his vehemence could not abide the delay of the canoe to carry him, but he rolled up his antique trowsers, and intrepidly went in on his shanks. He waded and splurged about promiscuously in the stream, which split and curled into riffles around his legs, as he moved or stood. Thereby he took a half dozen unwary trout, but probably terrorized all the others thereabouts. High, doubtless, was somewhat infected with Pratt's fever, but he preferred to indulge his more calculating and better regulated avidity dry-shod. He struggled along the bank, and chose a foothold on a stranded log, whence, with spendthrift prodigality, he thrashed away with his rod and line some time, but with only a single troutling captured..

High took this pitiful outcome with stoic calmness, and fell back on his blanket and literature. Denison sensibly utilized the spare time by stretching out in the shade, and snoozing innocently but not quite silently. I paid blissful tribute of greeting to the river of trout, and to the winds and skies that had graciously prospered us nearly all the way, in liberal oblations of burning incense of Havana from the meerschaum. Now that, like far-come Argonauts within sight of the golden fleece, our goal was at hand, and we could speedily reach out the hand and grasp the prize, we were content and tranquil. At eleven o'clock, the flotilla and its lading were in order for setting out for business. We stepped in, and then were joyously "afloat, afloat on the dark rolling tide" of the Brulè.

The limpid currents ran either gurgling musically over the shallows, or purling into eddies round an up-reared boulder, or shivering into sparkling ripples of tumult and riot on the rapids, or smoothing and lapsing into a reach of midsummer languor and faintness, but always pure, fresh and living, bearing in their forest-shaded course the chillness of the springs and founts that fed them so unattempered of the sun as to give always a grateful draught for thirst when dipped in the drinking-cup. This was the Brulé of our first experience—everywhere gravelled, rocky and bouldered, the very exclusive haunt and realm of trout, not like the Michigami or the Trout or Paint, with chubs and perch mingling in the population of fins.

We could now halt the pinnaces, almost at any place, from time to time, and were sure of a liberal spoil; and, after holding up for some of these interim casts, we had gradually and idly sauntered to a point estimated to be about twenty-eight miles above the mouth of the river, where we prospected a most eligible camping place. It was on a bank, embowered by a grove of largest cedars and pines, with gentle slopes of surface, free of troublesome undergrowth, the ground velveted and elastic with layers of twigs, with abundant shade, plenty of fuel and a wealth of hemlock boughs for the ground-spread of the tents. We named it Cedar Camp. We expected to make it a stopping place for two or three days, and could sally out from it up and down, and range all the pools and fishing places within easy reach. We could run the canoes light and quickly, and flit about at will.

The sport began auspiciously. A little over an hour's throwing produced a count of fifty, and, richly tinted and embrowned with the touches of the flame, they bountifully garnished the dinner platters in less than an hour, and ministered luxuriously to waiting appetites. The two hours following the feast were spent in camp in various modes of indolent and trivial leisure and laziness. No exertion more serious than that of fitting a ring on a rod, or burnishing a reel, or charging and fumigating with a pipe, or shifting a position on a blanket from an intrusion of the sun, was suffered to perturb the ease and delicious torpor of the situation.

Toward evening piscatorial aspirations revived. High and Pratt went below, and Denison and I breasted the tide upwardly. The fishing was of the best. To cast a fly upon the water was nearly a certainty of enticing a trout. In the first half-hour out, we could forecast the whole story of the sport on the Brulé. It was only to hold at any chance spot, to find that our lines would be cast in places pleasant for us. The throw on the one side or the other, from the canoe, was equally lucky. The trout appeared populous in every direction. Rises were bewilderingly plentiful. We needed reconnoisance but a short way from the camp to find the swimmers in force and voracity. So we soon returned with laden baskets, and turned over the abundance, or rather, the supplies brought in, to the cooks; for the surplus, beyond the needs of the fry, was tossed back into the water. At supper, we all expressed regrets that it was not in our power to bestow on friends at home, part of the excess of our lavish supply. But here, as elsewhere, and otherwise, one man's waste is another man's want.

Denison here evinced symptoms of a Minnesota chicken-shooting fever. He had arranged at Chicago to meet a friend for a gun-and-dog ramble for prairie hens. Shooting on the wing is his speciality. He would prefer dropping a few brace of pinnated grouse, on the rise, even to knocking a deer off its pegs. He had forwarded, in custody of the American express company, his retriever, Dick, in bond, to Minnesota. Probably the faithful dog had already chafed impatiently in his chain, and howled over his unfriended coercion in the leash, or had piteously bayed the moon for the lack of a job more suited to his training, and was, doubtless, then eagerly snuffing all the airs that blow in those windy latitudes for a scent of his master's coming. It was only a question of time when Denison would follow his thoughts to the dog and the grouse.

Our dash for trout was not so eager, now that they swam closely and superfluously. We slept late in the morning, and were not embarked for a take of a dinner mess before ten o'clock. During the night the minks played a sneak-thief game on us, by pilfering every trout from the fish-pans, and, in the few score of dressed fish, they laid by, in one night's fat work of theft, in their neighboring hole, a gorge of trout, for a prolonged gluttinous saturnalia of feasting. We were, therefore, troutless for breakfast, and to avenge the wholesale sack and plunder, it was resolved that dead-falls should be set for the scurvy pillagers. So traps were constructed and placed by the Indians, and, from the first of the next catch of trout, the most luscious and plump of the capture were affixed to the triggers. We gloated with much satisfaction on imagined minks entrapped, and fancied we should certainly see " with gripe tenacious held, the felons grin and struggle, but in vain."

When we next went out the trout were lively in their jumping to the throw, but they were less keen to take the fly. It seemed more in sport than in hunger that they leaped and leaped again; at all events, we were not brilliantly successful. Only forty were caught by the whole party; but as enough was as good as a feast, or for a feast, and having such a reasonable catch, we spent only an hour on the water. This essay of the rods exhausted, for the time, the party's vim. Tiring of killing trout, we devoted all our capacity of sloth to the problem of killing time indolently and inertly. We drowsily sat or reclined in the shade sunk in languor; we were not up to the mark of the usual dinner gusto. After the somewhat insipid repast, we betook ourselves to the tent for a siesta; but swarms of buzzing house-flies hungrily pricked us and drove us out.

High betook himself to a mammoth cedar and supported it by leaning against its mossy roots, in its shade, as serenely as Tityrus *recubans* under the beech tree, an impersonation of goneness and content, and was apparently lapsing into a deep reverie. A couple of minks, possibly in a freak of hilarity over their rich nocturnal plunder, scampered near by him playfully gamboling and squealing, and startled him from his meditation. This vivacity was a saucy presumptuousness provoking and great enough, on the instant, to rouse Denison's martial dander. He seized his gun and reconnoitered the bushes on tiptoe. Several minutes of fruitless watching cooled down his indignant fervency, and, disarming, he became a peaceable citizen again. Pratt's dudgeon, on account of the meagreness of the matinal repast caused by the felonious ravages of the minks, had not even yet subsided. He, therefore, armed and posted himself in the bushes with a finger on the trigger ready to execute sanguinary justice. He stood guard patiently, so long too, in his watching and biding his time, as to satisfy us that patience was one of his cardinal virtues.

This, his virtue, like virtue generally, finally proved its own reward. One of the minks furtively poked his head out of the hole to take a sly look around. Of the same head nothing more was ever known, either by the mink or the man. Without any official report from Pratt, we knew the effect of the shot by the smell that was instantly wafted into all the noses in the camp. When the Indians skinned and dismembered the mink in a *post mortem* examination, our sense of retributive justice was satisfied when a trout mess was found in the villain's viscera. In the sunset, we made brief essay with the rods. It was a stirring time, and our lines were kept musically whizzing in a shower of casts, when the flies pattered like raindrops.

# CHAPTER XV.

THE DEAD-FALL—A PORCUPINE GORMANDIZER—TRIALS OF A TROUTER—PATIENCE AND NOT PROFANITY—LITTLE BRULE FALLS—DENISON'S DOG—A THREATENED DUCKING—SUNDAY AIRS—PRATT AND THE MINKS AGAIN—NEW CAMP—BOOT LAKES—KAQUOTASH'S REMINISCENCES—A PINE RIVER BEAR ADVENTURE.

THE schemes of Indians, as well as of men and mice, "gang aft aglee." Kaquotash's well-laid deadfall, lusciously set with trout, was a failure by a large majority. Pratt's shot demoralized the minks, and, if they ventured out of their holes and hiding places, it was only on the sly, and the crafty stealers gave the snare a wide berth; they were, doubtless, plethoric with a gorge of feasting on their pillage of the night before, and they could afford to turn up their cunning noses and wag tails of contempt at the solitary *salmo fontinalis* impaled in the dead-fall. The early riser, though, surprised a happy porcupine squatted on the keel of an upturned canoe, exercising his jaws in browsing on a packing strap; he had already gnawed it lamentably, and if not then caught in his chew, would probably have devoured the whole leather. He made off and retreated with some alacrity, for one of his kind, up a tree. It was not with malice aforethought or in a mood of blood-thirstiness, but as a matter of strict justice that his life was made to pay the forfeit, though five revolver shots were required to give him a retributory quietus.

Unluckily Denison, while in a high tide of prosperous angling, fractured his rod in two places. He preserved an exemplary degree of equanimity over the casualty. If any one thinks it is not a perturbing *contretemps*, or a strain on the temper, to snap a rod, or by a luckless fling to twine the hackle into a limb, or tangle and kink the oil-silk line, or foul it with the other fellows' line, or lose a leader, just when the sport is in full play and the trout are skipping and flurrying the liveliest, he knows but little of an angler's mishaps and of the trials and contingencies that await him. No one has more frequent occasion for the exercise of all Christianly patience and forbearance than each of the eager sportsmen in a canoe cracking whips of rod and line in a trout stream.

It is a tolerably well disciplined temper that can steady itself evenly, and maintain composure and patience during a recurrence of such provoking casualties, and leave the trouter unmoved, so that he can as "a man whose blood is warm within, sit like his grandsire cut in alabaster." A good many of his disciples may remember Walton's advice to anglers—"Be patient, and forbear swearing, lest they be heard and catch no fish." The teaching is good, but it is not every one who has the grace to heed it. Denison, however, was guiltless of imprecations, and, like a disarmed soldier, useless in the field, retired quietly to the rear. He and Pratt evinced both their skill and patience in tinkering up and mending the fractures; they did it so neatly and successfully, that they protested the rod was really better than before, and it seemed, in fact, to verify the claim, and I seriously doubted if I had not better smash my own rod, and let them make it, too, better than it was in its first estate.

Reluctantly we struck the tents and left Cedar Camp, the most pleasant of our green-wood homes. On the downward way, we halted at points to fish; the trout leaped briskly, and at more than one of the stoppages, we were busied to unhook the captured. The sport was an *embarrass du richesses* of which the most ardent of the party began to tire. In the hour and a half of actual casting in these random exploits, a hundred and thirty were taken. Some of the trout are voracious; one that Pratt caught had been chewing a cud of fish, for a smaller one was in his throat not wholly swallowed. Along a considerable stretch the trees, on both sides, seemed nearly all to have fallen or grown into or toward each other, across the stream, as if in a friendly embrace of limbs, and it was, sometimes, a close and nice operation for us to pass through and under the intertwining arches of rich foliage. This overreaching forest tapestry only partially sheltered us from the pourings of a heavy thunder shower, whose flying squadrons of cloud swept over us.

When the massive columns of the storm had charged past, we laid in at Little Brulé Falls, to dry and to dine. We were in the full reality of the piscatorial condition named in the proverb of a fisherman's luck—wet breeches and a hungry stomach. As if almost a work of magic, a camp fire was ablaze with many tongues of flame and curls of smoke, so that the evaporation of our costumes and the process for the dinner went well on apace. When the kettle bubbled and the trout were fried, we plied the cups and forks with a relish and a will few diners and lunchers in the city ever realize. We felt princely after resting and dining. Perhaps Denison was an exception to the general condition of beatitude; he seemed a shade pensive, possibly from reveries about Dick the dog in Minnesota, or perchance some object dearer, at Chicago or elsewhere. We had the customary early afternoon lounge. . I enjoyed the situation simply by lying at rest, watching the quivering of the leaves, listening to the chattering of the red squirrels or the lulling music of the water foaming over the rocks.

The falls, so-called, are an insignificant pitch of the river, a few feet over ledges of rock; they are something of precipitous rapids, rather than a cascade. Toward evening when the canoes were manned for fishing, the one carrying High and Denison, lurched into a swirl near the drop of the falls, and was nearly sucked under, shipped water considerably and seemed on the verge of swamping; but Paul was just quick and skillful enough, by a masterly handling of the pole, to poise and right her into equilibrium again and shove her out of peril. During the imminency of the catastrophe, the legal gentlemen were, evidently, for the moment, vertebrally affected with frigid sensations; they were, at least, threatened with a sousing bath, and their skins escaped drenching by just a hair-breadth excess of good fortune.

Along in the night, while we palefaces were, or should have been, sleeping and dreaming, the native Americans were having their own pleasantries in their tent. Their laugh and jabber told a tale of jovial good spirits, and waked unwonted echoes in the solemn cloisters of the woods; they enjoyed their part of the programme, not less than we enjoyed ours; their night's sleep is usually preluded with a merry pow-wow, and fun all to themselves.

Whatever muscularity they have exerted during the day, either in packing over the carries, or navigating the flotilla, or doing varied utility business in the camp, there was always time for their lively palaver and smoking, before " o'er their brows death counterfeiting sleep with leaden and batty wings did creep." Were we ever the theme of their jokes and pleasantries? We knew not. None but a philologist, learned in the dialect of the Menominees, could tell. As Montaigne said about the playing with the cat, who knows whether the cat was most amused at the man, or the man at the cat? Who of us could say if we were objects of more diversion to them than they appeared odd and amusing to us? However that may be, these invaluable red fellows, the primitive copperheads, had then been long enough in our service, and so thoroughly in harmony of will and spirit with us, that we considered them admitted to full membership in our forest brotherhood.

In the matter of costume, our outfit for more than the simplest changes, bordered close on the vocative; the Sunday toilette was but slightly different from the secular raiment. For instance, Pratt made some pretension to style by scraping his beard to a closer stubble, and by a fresh collar to his neck. High wiped his lips with an unprecedented napkin at breakfast, and effected an innovation by turning the sleeve-cuffs of his brown linen shirt out in full flow; Denison made a clean breast of it by buttoning his vest up to the throat. I took on a silk neckerchief knotted into a nondescript tie. These touches of the elegant were not particularly apt to inspire much pride of the flesh or lust of the eye, but symbolically or typically, they were just as good as if tip-top.

We were tired of Little Brulé Falls, and as a Sunday work of charity to ourselves, packed up, loaded and embarked for ongoing. As downward meant, with Denison, Minnesota, dog and grouse, we were every mile nearing the place, and every hour nearing the time of separation and of a break in our fraternal cohesion. The prospect of near disorganization imparted something of a serious tone, rather in harmony with Sabbath decorum.

Yet, after all, the *carpe diem* spirit was not wanting. It moved Pratt to prove himself no exception to the rule of appetite growing with what it feeds on. Having had a taste of blowing off a mink's head, a mania for minks possessed him. He determined to lay in armed preparation for them as we passed the banks, on the way. He took the forward canoe, and had his gun in hand, well slugged for deadly work among the vermin, and kept a patient, keen lookout. Scarcely a twig rustled on either side, or a dark root protruded, or a trout plunged, or a stir was heard in the bushes, that he was not ready to make prompt and short work of it. And so we passed on and on, down smooth reaches, turning bends, past clumps and bushes, log drifts, shaded pools, twining roots, sandy strips of beach, and all places where minks might be expected. But his watching was unrewarded, and even his cardinal virtue of patience gave out, and his futile vigilance became tediously monotonous. Either because they kept to their holes on Sundays, or from an instinct of Pratt's hostile machination, it was certainly a bad day or an off-day for minks.

At noon we laid to on the Michigan side, to camp. Fronting the spot was a little island clothed with a mass of alders; on the opposite shore beyond it, was our camping place of before the head of the trail to Boot lakes. It is a low, marshy ground; but our new camping was now on a high, dry bank. It was overshadowed by the most umbrageous of forests; the bushes were soon cleared by the axe, and a convenient area of lawn-like smoothness was converted into a choice and pleasant tenting place. The canvass was set up; the kettle was hung; the frying pan told its tale of crisping and browning trout. The repast was grateful and needed. In the post-prandial divan on the grass, we put it into our pipes and smoked it how to make the afternoon available. A pilgrimage to Boot lake, or lakes rather, was hinted and then considered in a *pourparler* of *pros* and *cons*.

There are three of these lakes, with a hard portage from the river to the nearest, and portages thence and between the others; but the question was settled, when it was known that there is a rumor of large trout in the further water, and the first lake is a noted resort for deer. The hearsay of the trout determined High, and the repute of the deer won Denison. The venture with the fly and the gun was therefore prepared for, and, as a stay over night was a necessity, an outfit of tent, commissary stores and canoe, was at once improvised. Thebault and Joe Dixon were the muscular auxiliaries and guides for the campaign. The four remaining signalized the start with a generous send-off of good wishes and huzzas.

As our supper had to be caught, Pratt and I took to the water to sway the rods awhile. Though we went not more than gunshot range from camp, the trout swarmed; the sport was exhilarating, and busied us to the extent of our capacity and exceeding the measure of our wishes. The capture figured up to ninety-three. The fish here, on the average, are smaller than the upper ones; but they make nearly as good sport, and are quite as savory for the meal as those taken above.

Kaquotash was in an unusually social and gossiping mood at night; his spirits enlivened into unwonted effervescence, and his volubility of speech, for an Indian, was something rare; his mind took an autobiographical turn. While the fire-light flickered and played in his face, and, at times softened or glowed on his swarthy features, his weird appearance, with his oddities of tongue, were a kind of sorcery which held us all willing and attentive subjects. Of course, the greater part of his life has been that of much forest wandering; he has been something of a sailor, too, and vividly related the foundering condition of a propeller which he piloted through a perilous Green Bay storm, finally into harbor.

Some experiences as a Wisconsin cavalryman in Georgia, in the war, showed that David was no slouch of a soldier, and that he had had hair-breadth escapes by field as well as by flood; but his adventures in the woods were the most amusing and entertaining of his recollections. In the course of nearly thirty years he has been over and over all these northern wildernesses, with locators, prospectors, surveyors of lands, and with hunters and fishers, and also as a logger, so that he is an authority on topographical, navigating, sporting, cooking, camping matters, as well as thoroughly versed in the natural history of the wilds, and their fish, flesh and fowl varieties.

A story of a round with a bear, on Pine River, was related to us. He and a white man undertook to capture a couple of bear cubs they saw in a tree. The parent brute was off foraging, probably; but by way of precaution against a sudden return of the dam, they built a girdle of fire around as an intended barrier of safety. When it was well ablaze, and David was about to climb, the mother came madly rushing through the brush toward them; their only weapon of defense was an axe; with this in his hand, David retreated backward as fast as the circumstances and his Indian legs would allow; the enraged bear rapidly advanced; the pallid white man precipitated himself, with marvelous strides, to the river, and leaped into the canoe, shoving it out into the stream, far and fast as he could, leaving Kaquotash in the lurch, bawling loudly as he went: "Get aboard, Dave, get aboard!"

By that time, the she-bear reared up on her haunches to grapple the Indian in her fatal embrace. Further backing was impossible. David stopped and stood his ground, with the axe drawn, looking the savage brute steadily in the eyes. The bear paused, too, motionless, for a few seconds, fixed by his moveless gaze, and then quailingly dropping on all fours, herself retreated, tail foremost to her cubs, and

"Cow'd and subdued, fled from the face of man,
Nor bore one glance of his commanding eye."

## CHAPTER XVI.

FORMER CAMP—ARBOREAL INSCRIPTIONS—THE BOOT LAKE PARTY—FISH MARVELS—A BEAR THAT WAS A BUGBEAR—TROUT JUMPING AND FROLICS—COMMITTEE OF THE WHOLE —GOOD-BYE TO DENISON—MORE FISHING—AN AQUEOUS AFTERNOON.

PRATT and I made a morning excursion with the canoe. We paddled over to our camping ground of before. There was very little of the *genius loci* to enthuse us. It was overgrown with weeds and grasses. It is a situation dismal enough. Some iconoclastic barbarian had ruthlessly, with an axe, chipped away the rude memorials we had inscribed on an unbarked surface of a tree to mark and commemorate our abiding there.

These arboreal inscriptions are customary at camping points. They answer to the hotel register as memoranda of travel and sojourn, and, by comity of wayfarers in the woods, are considered as sacredly privileged from spoliation as the legends sculptured on a grave-yard monument. The catches of fish are often arithmetically etched on these tree-tablets, and sometimes these, as also names and dates, are inscribed in rare vagaries of figures and writing.

The little spring rill, which purely and coldly trickled, and which was the only satisfying natural feature of the place, was now choked up and hidden by weeds. We recalled reminiscences of the spot, and then willingly turned our direction from it. We thence cruised down the stream, and skirmished here and there with the rods, and relieved the Brulé of thirty-seven of its enamelled beauties; we skirmished about leisurely more for an airing than for sporting. Getting back to camp we found our pilgrims returned from their overland wandering; they had a good deal more to tell of than to show, for their digression to the lakes of Boot. All they brought in was a brace of partridges, the plump and glossy victims of Denison's gunning.

They brought the recollections, not the carcass of a deer, seen in a safe perspective of distance, which the deer was wary and witting enough to keep from being foreshortened; they had portaged over the canoe for a night hunt with the lantern; they coasted the curving borders of the lake, stealing noiselessly through the tall grasses in the shallows, or cutting a swathe among the lily pads, or skimming gently over the still clear water, with the glare of the light casting a glittering refulgence ahead, they themselves and their canoe thrown in shadow and concealment.

But there was no sight or sound of a deer, no rustle in the bushes, and no stir in the water. The night hunt was a failure; though that was not singular, and not at all unexpected. The night was bright; Luna had put on her brightest face, such as that with which she shone loveliest to meet and woo her Endymion alone on the mountain and encircle him in her golden halo; there was no playing or laying a successful ambuscade in the streaming rays of the moon; consequently, Denison's venison, which was to garnish our refections, was only moonshine.

The stories they told of the bass, in the further lake, were those of icthyological wonders; the water was clear as crystal, and the lake a natural aquarium, with transparency enough to reveal the thick shoals of fish disporting beneath; they were seen fearlessly swimming in hordes; the place is stocked with them, as if there was no limit to their indefinite spawning and propagation; they darted about at random, without fear of foes or danger on the surface. The lake is seldom visited; an angler who can have his utmost fill of sport, that which is the superlative of all sport, in abundance, at least, on the Brulé, is scarcely apt to venture the trying ordeal of the rough trails over there, to squander time in the muscular exertion of heavy pulling and dragging out which bass fishing is. So the Boot lake bass are not decimated or thinned out by fishers. Our party took thirty or more of them, mainly by trolling.

High was heedless enough to try his delicate trout rod, and one of the heavy weights nipped his fly, and the tug was so strong that his slender tip snapped like a pipe-stem. Denison dropped in a spoon, with a flaming red pendant, and dangled it near the surface and said that a concourse of all-sized bass loomed up in a circle around it, and poised there on their fins, a sort of wondering, gaping throng around his glaring bob. As a Master in Chancery, who swears others to tell the truth, ought himself to be truthful, we accepted this relation as truth and nothing but the truth; though a considerable story of fish, it was not, he affirmed, a fish story. The fish they caught would weigh from five pounds down to one; they soon tired of their miraculous draught of fishes, went ashore, and, like Arabs, silently folded their tent and stole wonderingly away.

There was a bear incident, also, at Boot lake, or bug-bear, or, only the bare imagination of a bear, and not a real bruin. In trailing to the lake, the party straggled on in Indian file, with Denison in the van, High, Thebault and Dixon bringing up the rear, at intervals; Frank then came suddenly to a dead halt, and excitedly reported "A bear! a bear!"

It was not told to us whether the hair electrically lifted on the scalps of the hunter and fisher; but, with rare presence of mind, under alarming circumstances, they discreetly abstained from a bold headlong dash, or instant onset on the dangerous enemy, and prudently waited the reinforcement of the experienced bear-slayers from the rear. "Where? where?" inquired Thebault and Dixon, looking grave, as they always do, when there is serious business on hand or foot, each cautiously scanning, on tip-toe, the direction pointed out by Denison.

When Denison succeeded in at length directing the Indian's vision point blank to the supposed bear, the natives simultaneously burst into a roar of laughter; of course, this completely demoralized and confounded the Chicago barristers. The Indians declared that the "bear was a porcupine!" and really, the savage bear of an unmitigated optical illusion was, after all, a bugaboo of a porcupine, of most harmless propensities, peacefully sunning itself on a charred stump!

> "Such tricks hath strong imagination,
> \* \* \* \* imagining some fear,
> How easy is a bush suppos'd a bear."

This ursine hallucination was one of the wonders of the Boot lake expedition about which our bamboozled comrades were not inclined to indulge in any sounding manifestoes.

Pratt and myself struck a choice trout lead, which we worked beautifully. The activities of the brilliant leapers were most varied in their displays; they almost literally flew about as if their fins for water were as well wings for the air. Sometimes the high-flyers, as if in play themselves, or as if striving in a grab or snatching match, would leap at once for the same fly. One of them vaulted over a log, as neatly as an expert tumbler would turn a bar; another would skip ducks and drakes along, bobbing in and out. This was all rather a comical piscatory pleasantry to us. David told us that the trout, going up creeks and small streams, make no bones of tossing over logs, and said he had seen a trout throw himself up over Brulé Falls, a good three feet jump. Seeing and hearing these gymnastical feats, I am not sure that it would have greatly surprised us to see a trout climbing a tree! It certainly would not have been wonderful for one to have flirted into the canoe. There is no end to the freaks of the volatile imps.

In the golden sunset, we meandered the twisting thread of the river back to the camp, cutting with the prow the silvery surface into ripples triangulating off to the edges, and swaying the grasses and the dipping leafage into waving motion. As the last faint red tinges of the sky faded into twilight, we reached the grassy quay of the camp-ground. That night, after the meal, when the pipes were suffusing, and after the drowsy autochthones had retired, the Chicago party resolved itself into a committee of the whole.

Denison and his outset for Minnesota were the special order of the day, and the subject of interpellation and debate. The fever for that remote promise-land of grouse was now a furor too imperative to be stayed or repressed. The rush of dog to the head must, we saw, inevitably lead to his taking off. And so Dick, off towards the north star, was too much for us all. We were ready to pronounce on the blameless cur, Launce's outlawry declared against the misbehaving Crab: "Out with the dog!" "Whip him out!" "Hang him up!" As the only mode of outgo was by canoe, the leaving would require a withdrawal of half the party, and a moiety of the equipment. Pratt volunteered to be his companion, though it was only a perfunctory assent given—a necessity more than a choice. It was left to the Indian contingent to settle for itself which of the guides should attend Denison. When so much of the programme was settled, it was late, and the committee rose, and having, like Bottom, "an exposition of sleep come upon" us, we took to the reposeful blankets, leaving the sweet sorrow of the parting for the rosy early hours of day.

Chickabiddy Camp, in the morning, was early and busily astir, for a goodly and timely starting and send-off of our parting comrades. Of course, we collectively felt, for the first time on the trip, emotions of regret as the time was come to word the farewell with the lips. In the boundless and overpowering presence and solitude of nature, our intimacy had grown so close, warm, united and sympathetic, that near fellowship became warm fraternity. Parting would be a break in our unity and community of spirit, and, though some of us should meet again in the city, our paths then would be too diverse, and our several preoccupations too varied to admit of the union into one continuing common mood and mind like that of the woods, where "the electric chain wherewith we are darkly bound" kept us constantly and vividly *en rapport*. We felt something of this on the eve of the dissolution. It was not embodied in lip-language.

In fact we rather affected facetiousness. But the mirth was like that sometimes intended to mask solemnity. It was not the real mirth that makes the side ache, and soothes away the hurt of heart-ache. Our jokes were too weighty to be witty. With them all there was one word we were loth to speak, that should be kept back to the last—"good-bye." We had found we were such good and right companions to be together, we felt we ought to keep the companionship unbroken to the end. And so, when the time came for us to loosen the silver chord, and sever our entirety into parting companies, we knew, those hasting and those loitering, that there would be an emotion deeper, truer and warmer than is found in a common-place adieu.

The guides shared these feelings. They were averse to breaking up. Neither of them wanted to be of the returning portion of the party. Which it should be at the last only was settled, as between David and Thebault, by casting lots; and it was the long twig drawn by Kaquotash that fated him to go. Shortly after eight o'clock, everything and everybody were ready, and the order "all aboard," given by Denison, signalled the last moment. The pressure of hands in the adieu was warm. And then in their birchen shell, the Tom King, Denison and David, Pratt and Joe Dixon, glided away in the distance. High and I recurred to the passage in Walton of the parting of Piscator and his companion, and applied his words on our occasion: "We are loth to part with you now, but when you tell us you must go, we will then wait upon you with our thoughts, all the miles of your way, and heartily wish you a good journey." For the kindly and thoughtful David Kaquotash, who had so well served us and so much attached us, he of the native and we of the foreign race and language, we uttered a fervent "God bless you!" We will wear in our hearts his living memory. Our aspiration was, may he live long and prosper, and when he dies may he go to the place where the good Indians go.

We thought the fitting thing by way of relief against the present sense of the loneliness and vacancy of the camp, was to divert our thoughts from it and our friends to the fish. To that end, we arranged the tackle in its best trim, and setting out on the Brulé, radiant in the glow of the morning, the birch bark we sat in, like Cleopatra's barge on the river of Cydnus, " a burnished throne, burned on the water," so glaring, at starting, was the dazzle of the sun.

We crept along the winding of the stream, from pool to pool, or through frothy shallows, or into a shadowed nook, or breasted the rapids, and also flung out at random while in transit. During the two or three hours of the coursing we caught only forty-five trout, but did catch a very brief, sudden, refreshing shower, from a single cloud that a wayward impromptu gust swept over us. On Sunday and the day following, the heat was something of the tropics, and at night we dispensed with the illumining and warming from the usual pine ingleside of the camp, and very comfortably enjoyed our last meerschaums before bedtime, in the midsummer night scene in shirt-sleeves. This balminess of the night hours, however, was a rarity and fitfulness of temperature. In this camp, and as if spawned or vitalized by the warmth, the houseflies plagued us fiendishly, more tormentingly than the mosquitoes or midgets.

The afternoon sport was dashed by rain, which fell copiously from serried cohorts of cloud that swept up, charging fiercely from the west. Part of the time it subsided into a glimmer or a mist of rain, and again showered heavily, so that we were embargoed by the elements into indoor listlessness. Looking out of the open flap of the tent, the prospect was dreary enough. The rain drops dotted and pimpled the stream thickly. They pelted and spluttered in the camp fire, and clipped its flames, and plumped and dully thudded among the embers and in the ashes, and the tongues of the blazes hissed and sizzled angrily in the strife of fire and water. The pines and firs dripped ceaselessly. The sky was leaden and sullen. Thebault and Paul took their enforced seclusion with the most happy go-lucky composure, laboriously whiffing their pipes and indolently sprawling on the blankets in their tent.

Against the outer dreariness and the inner monotony we fell back on our literature for relief. In his consuming thirst for information about that "Mysterious Island" of Jules Verne, and between the book and his pipe, High forgot, possibly, the clouds, the rain, the dullness, the general discomfort of the occasion. I turned the pages of honest Walton, and following his footsteps on the banks of the river Lea, for the time was unmindful of the very Brulé at our feet, and, in those charming discoursings which have made the "Complete Angler" forever a lovable classic in our language, renewed some of those sweet spells which fascinated me in earlier years. We had time, too, to speak of our away-gone friends, and of course we missed Denison's restless volatility.

Some of Denison's equipment we could willingly afford to part withal. One familiar object, whose room was greatly preferred to its company, was his portable powder magazine, which he called an ammunition case. This twenty-five pound locker of deadly missiles was generally lying around in the tent for us to stumble our toes against, or to menace some, or all of us, with an explosive hoist, to the "demnition bow-wows." It was about as safe and cheerful a companion to have around as a torpedo or a carboy of dynamite, when lighted meerschaums were so freely swung around, and the sparks, like whirling myriads of fire-flies, were flying in showers from our breakfast fires, dinner fires, supper fires, and our morning and evening tent fires. That ammunition case must have been the terror of the men, if for no other reason than that of its being a heavy dorsal strain on every Indian whose unhappy fate it was to lug it on the portages. The fixed ammunition, as he termed his cartridges, never was fixed, apparently, as he seemed constantly fixing it. He handled it freely, as a child would play its rattles and baubles. His case was opened as often as the valise that held his novels. Nobody could tell when an ill-governed or wayward spark might be the means of blowing up the camp, and all who dwelt therein. He appeared to think his explosives had a useful disciplinary purpose in schooling us to sleepless vigilance and caution.

He spread out a two-pound package of powder on a newspaper on the grass in front of the tent, to dry in the sun. He emphatically warned me to be careful about smoking, as I might drop a spark in his powder, and blow up the entire stock and spoil his shooting. The admonition, certainly, was so apt and timely, and so well meant for the safety of the powder, if not of myself, that I felt grateful for his cautionary kindness, and was rather inclined to consider him my benefactor. In looking around for marks to shoot at, he discovered a wasp's nest suspended from a limb of a tree near the tent. He thought that, by right of discovery, he was privileged to deal with it in his own way, and that was to shatter it into flinders with his revolver. It was all I could do to keep him from blowing it into fragments and setting loose on us the whole swarm of infuriated wasps, to make it hot and lively around the camp. He seemed to regard the obnoxious vespiary as a hanging provocation or challenge for his revolver marksmanship. Sitting under or near it, he was uneasy and perturbed, like Damocles beneath the suspended sword at the Dyonisian feast.

I am not sure that he forgave, or ever will quite forgive me for thwarting him of the ecstacy of demolishing that wasp's nest into everlasting atoms.

At twilight the rain increased, and it was by a bare excess of the chances that the kitchen fire was not squelched, and we were not sent supperless to bed. By chipping and splintering dry pine, chopped from the under sides of logs, the Indians found just enough fuel to keep combustion alive; and though the drops pattered on the kettle, the water within at last boiled into a bubbling song of tea. The fire for our tent drowned out, and the night darkness and dampness crept on us. The gloom within was made more conspicuous by the weak, uncertain flare of the lantern suspended. To shut out the utter dismalness of the outside, and to close ourselves in, the flaps of the tent were drawn together, the tallow dip, our flickering glim, was put out, and, in the blankets, we gradually soothed away and lost the miseries of the situation in sleep.

# CHAPTER XVII.

SKIRMISHING FOR FISH—A RED TROUT—CRASSUS THE ROMAN—A RARE DISH—RIVER RISE—ECCENTRIC FREAKS OF FISH—A LUNAR EFFECT—THE SAW-BILLS—RED SQUIRRELS—INDIANS TROUTING—A COLOSSAL TROUT—HIGH, THE CHAMPION ANGLER.

THE clouds that lowered on our house the last night, were in the deep bosom of the ocean buried. In the morning we woke to a very resplendence of sunshine; the azure was without even the fleck of a cloud; the green of the forest was a deeper emerald; the air was pure and laden with the odors of balsam. We were in the best of spirits, though we missed some of the boisterous fun or chaffing with which we had been wont to welcome in the jocund morn. We wished Pratt and Denison were with us for our and their own longer pleasure in the sports of the Brulé. After the first order of the day, the breakfast, was disposed of, the business next in order was proceeded with. The splendid morning incited us to an excursion on the river, now, after the gloom and sulleness of the previous day, more than ever attractive in its fullness of summer glories.

> "Now let the fisherman his toils prepare,
> And arm himself with ev'ry wat'ry snare;
> His hooks, his lines peruse with careful eye,
> Increase his tackle, and his rod re-tie."

It needed all Paul's exertions to push the craft up the stiff currents swollen with the rains. At times, it was heaving ahead very slowly. At various pools, where we held awhile, we most prosperously whipped the stream. Our concern was, not to hover where the trout swarmed most abundantly, but to find the haunts of the largest. The small fry could be plenteously caught in nearly any place of the river; but the heavy swells, more shy and wary, frequent under a bank where the water runs close up and deep, or under logs, or in deep pools or holes, or at or under the rapids, or in the depths of the channel, or in the swirl below a large boulder. They are more coy than the troutlings, and sometimes must be coaxed and tickled with a delicate and cautious dalliance.

We happened on some of these haunts of the choice fish. Right gallantly did they show the gamesome stuff of which they were made. There was agitation in the waters when they stretched a line and bent a tip. I envied High the repeated onset and final capture of one particular trout, splendid in his mettle and dash, and in his proportions and unequalled beauty. On his first charge at the fly, he appeared, in the clear water, a flash of deep, red flame, so brilliant was he in his emblazonry; but he was not then taken. On the next cast he pitched at the fly as it touched the water. We thought him taken, and saw him wavering in shape of red as he was being played in; but, after all, he flouted off and we thought him gone forever. But fate had set its seal on him; on a third immediate cast, he came boldly to the snatch again, and then he was firmly struck.

How slowly, carefully and skillfully High handled his rod so as to save his gallant, struggling prize. When he was being drawn in, fluttering and writhing, he appeared to us as if reddened in his own blood. He fought gamely to the last. When brought in and unhooked, each of us took him, by turns, and handled him tenderly, and with wonder and admiration at his beauty. He was the sole one of the kind we had ever seen taken from the Brulé. He was peerless in size as he was in brilliancy. The tail, fins and belly were of deepest red. The specks were unusually defined and high colored, and the skin was finely empearled and perfect. We all regretted that he could not be kept alive or preserved to be taken home as a wonder. He would be a marvel of beauty in a parlor aquarium or fish globe.

He was a paragon of a trout, handsome enough to be kept and fondled as a pet, as was the lamprey of Crassus, the orator, which would come at his call and feed from his hand. That eminent Roman forensic gentleman wept when his fondling of the pond died. His tears occasioned a repartee of his, which Ælian has been thoughtful enough to preserve, and which shows that it was a great point with the lawyers of the Roman, as it is with those of the modern forum, to have the last word. Ænobarbus was the colleague of the orator in the censorship, and foolhardily ventured to twit his brother official on his puling and sobbing over a defunct fish. The legal wit retorted that it was not for Domitius Ænobarbus to taunt Licinius Crassus with bewailing anything, since the same Domitius had buried three wives without rending his toga or tearing his beard, and without a single tear or whimper at the funeral of either demised consort, or words to that effect. As the historian has not reported a reply, it is to be presumed that the widowered Roman silently withered.

As a *dernier resort*, and the only one, the beauty-trout was handed over to the cook for his professional treatment. It was served at our *table d' hote*, and, at High's special instance, fell to my platter. Beneath his crisp and embrowned coat of mail, the tender flakes were delicate and sweet, and of the deepest pink salmon tinge, and were as choice to eat as fair to look upon. It was a dainty dish, of which it could be said, as Walton says of a service of fish described by him, it was "too good for any body but anglers and very honest men."

In the afternoon, and after our customary lounge in the shade, we put off for further essaying with the fly. The rain of the night before, by that time, had swollen the river more voluminously so that it ran swiftly smooth over ordinary shallows. It was all channel. The canoe could float about anywhere, and we could strike trout around about us nearly everywhere. Just at the camp, too, we could take them. At the rapids lower down, where Pratt and I had fortuned on a paying lead, as the miners say, we failed to get a rise, probably because the water swept too turbulently. This convinced us, what indeed, was believed before, that the fish are wandering, and do not shoal in pools when there is waterway to swim them freely at large. In the Brulé at its full stream, the trout are wanderers—here to-day, and to-morrow elsewhere.

We saw some of their amusing freaks again; one voracious fellow vaulted over a log to snatch a fascinating, new, glossy fly that High had thrown, and did tackle it, but paid dearly for the leap, for he was captured, and was plump enough to be laid by as a choice morsel for the pan. Another trout skipped horizontally, at least two feet along, barely above and in line with the surface, and then frisked out sideways and dropped back flat into the water laterally. These antics rather amazed and much amused us. The figures of the day were one hundred and sixty-five.

I got up in the night to close the flaps of the tent, and witnessed a striking lunar effect. Fog was dense over the river. The moon, directly opposite to, or fronting the camp, shone lustrously; a narrow pathway of illuminated golden haze stretched from the brink, at our feet, in rising perspective, up to the face of the moon. Early in the morning, when the glories of the coming day were glimmering the east into the hues of dawn, the flock of saw-bills that ill-omened our Michigami voyage, or some others of the nefarious family, were heard quacking and seen paddling in the very purview of the camp. One of the boys rising from his snore frightened them, and as usual they boisterously scattered in terror.

There was a settlement of small red squirrels around us. They were very nimble, and the trees near by were noisy with their lively chattering. They ventured occasionally on the trees overhanging the camp. One of them capered neatly on alder bushes within twenty feet of us, bending down slender branches, swinging from one to another, swaying on twigs, rattling the leaves, and whisking his tail. We saw several of them chasing, one after another, in a jumping race, on logs, squeaking sharply as they went. There were small birds, like sparrows, flitting among the bushes in hide-and-go-seek playfulness, twittering little trills.

A chipmunk sometimes came, and stopped on a log to take a look at us. Occasionally the croak of a raven, or the moan of a loon high flying, the rat-tat of a sapsucker, or the pecking of a woodpecker, or the jerking notes of a jaybird, and some other notes not familiar to us, were heard, and proved that bird-life is more varied and abundant here than on the Michigami; but even here the feathered choristers were not, either in number or variety, what would be expected in such a grand old wilderness. High was thoughtful enough of the better-half serving the household gods at home, to gather and press for her in the leaves of a Jules Verne extravaganza, some of the choicest of the ferns, which mantled the ground near by with a livery of vivid green.

We ourselves prompted Thebault and Paul to experiment their Indian skill in a match with the trout. Whether or not they would be successful with the fly and our more delicate appliances, who had only occasionally trouted, and then, with ruder line, and rod fashioned from a branch and with bait, was a problem they themselves had no experience from which to forecast results at starting. We committed to them our rig, and they canoed upwardly, and, in their venture, wielded the rods so much to the purpose, in their dalliance with the fish, as to return to us with flying colors and with fifty-three trout, news of which they proudly hailed to us as they rounded to the mooring. Whether this, their first foraging the river, had edged their appetites more sharply, or whether they had a special relish because the spoils were of their own capture, we did not know, but certainly they bountifully served themselves and repeated more than their usual courses of the fry.

After dinner, we set out again to fish. From some whim or caprice, in quest of novelty, and to variegate our bearings, we pushed into untried inlets, unexplored nooks and unknown chutes. We tried one or two openings into the stream, which in short time we found to be *culs de sac* of water in which we were entrapped, and were obliged to turn about and retrace our course. Within a short distance of the camp there are numerous little islands, with threads of stream tangling and winding about them, Venetian-like petty lagoons. Into one of these, High's prying curiosity prompted a venture; after we ascended some distance from the entrance, it so narrowed and crooked, the foliage so overstretched it, the snags, sunken brush and fallen timber so obstructed the passage, that it was hard to force the birch-bark on, though Paul struggled manfully. But we had pressed on so far that to return were as tedious as to go on. We determined to crowd ahead to the main stream

A few pushes further, at a point where seemingly there was no promise of a fish of any size, High instinctively caught sight of a narrow, dark strip of water, close under a shore, embanked by a dense luxuriance of alders, and carefully laid in his fly, on a short piece of line. It was, except to an eye of faith, a forlorn hope of a place. There was no space for two to cast. But the chance dip of the fly proved, by a rise, that the hidden spot might be a lair of trout. The hint was followed up, and its promise was followed too, by splendid performance.

Again casting his fly at the very shore-line in the dark strip, its touch on the water was one as of magic, and proved to be the master-stroke of all Brulé fly-fishing. He had struck a trout that tried his tackle and his skill. His rod curved, the reel buzzed, and the line spun out taut down stream. To prevent the fish from loosening, or from fouling the line in the brush and logs, was the critical and turning point. Gay must have had, or seen a similar match with a trout, as in his "Rural Sports," he foreshadows High in what was nearly literally a brush with the Brulé trout, differing only in the mightiness of the bulk and unfolded length. As thus—

> Now hope exalts the fisher's beating heart;
> Now he turns pale and fears his dubious art;
> He views the trembling fish with lonigng eyes,
> While the line stretches with th' unwieldy prize;

> Each motion humors with his steady hands,
> And one slight hair the mighty bulk commands;
> Till tired at last, despoiled of all his strength
> The game athwart the stream unfolds his length.

Paul and I anxiously watched the gallant tourney, and were one in admiration over the prize. It was the leviathan or monarch trout of the Brulé—larger than any known to, or heard of by any of us taken on this river. We could fairly weight him at two pounds. The average of the larger trout taken in this river, or by us, was probably not over fourteen ounces. High was tickled almost into boyish exhilaration at his capture. What a volley of admiring exclamations he uttered! What a serene expression and halo of smiles he wore; how often he spoke of him, and how many times he opened the basket to be sure he was there, as though, like Falstaff chuckling over the fallen Percy, he soliloquized: "What if he should rise again?" and renew the fight anon, I cannot undertake to note. I know he said that he felt better on the taking of the trout than if he had taken a successful verdict in a Chicago law suit;

> "And all the day an unaccustomed spirit
> Lifts him above the ground with cheerful thoughts."

This will be the red-letter day in High's calendar of Brulé trouting. The rest of the angling was rather tame to him. Though the fish we afterwards took were considerably above the average, they seemed to him, after the splendid trout *coup de grace*, rather puny. The peerless one took the dash out of his ambition. In fact, our sport, in weight and number, was so good that he said that, for once, he had had all the trouting he wanted, which, for an irrepressible enthusiast of fly-fishing, as he is, was a rare confession. We took one hundred and fifty, but returned most of them to the river again. The day was the finest in breeze and sunshine, the evening was cool and still, the unclouded moonlight tinged all the landscape in yellow glow. We felt genial as the warmth of the log-fire and bright as its flames, and were as placid and blissful as if everything was, and would remain, as serene as the night.

## CHAPTER XVIII.

CHICKABIDDY CAMP—HARPING ON THE TROUT—RIVER RECEDING—A FAWN AND A BUCK—CHANGE IN THE BRULE——CAMP THEBAULT—THE TOTAL FIGURES—LOGMAN'S CAMP—THE MICHIGAMI— WEAWBINYKET'S CABIN—PAUL MILLER'S—BIG QUINISECK FALLS.

THEBAULT thought, perhaps, a day as propitious as that which saw the killing of the splendid trout, should be crowned with more than wonted comfort for the night, so he hewed down a towering hemlock standing near the camp, and despoiled it of a wealth of boughs to make us a fresh and fragrant spread for sleeping. These made a couch as much to our ease, if not quite as soft, as feathers could make.

The balmy sleep, which was there our tired nature's sweet restorer was deep as the slumber of infancy in the cradle. No one so well knows what it is to sleep in peace and wake in joy, as well as to have good digestion wait on appetite, and health on both

—where appetite is ever under the spur or on edge—as the roamer in this forest realm of nature, of solitude and of calm.

Enamored of our camping place, we had thought to make there a longer stay; but the water-rise was running out rapidly, and the trout would be less scattered and broadcast. Besides, it was reported that certain of the stores were exhausted, and others were depleting rapidly. The prospect of famine had expedited the return on the first trip. As we were now cloyed with excess of sport, and of satiety "a little more than a little is much too much," we would be making no great sacrifice in emigrating from Chickabiddy Camp.

High was still harping on his notable trout. I do not know what his war record is, but I doubt if any single event of it, in the field, on the march or in camp, will be a more satisfying recollection to him than that of his conquest of the mammoth trout. Of course, compared with the three, four or five pound trout, or salmon trout which he himself had captured from Rocky Mountain streams, the Brulé captive would be dwarfed and overshadowed; but here, where the scale is reduced, and the fish make up in dash, gameness, beauty and delicacy, what they lack in dimensions and weight, to have proved himself the unrivaled master of the rod, with an unmatched marvel of its kind for a trophy, was indeed a feat and good fortune worth emblazoning on his piscatorial escutcheon.

His superb trout, however, fried, and in a crust of brown, was served in a breakfast mess. And, much of a trout *gourmet* as he is, High had all he could do to get away with it. He exercised his jaws with a gusto and with a labor of love in disposing of the rich, delicate, creamy flakes, akin to those of the stomach attributed to a hungry Feejee epicure for a missionary tid-bit. I could not muster assurance enough to accept the slice of it offered to me. After rising from the feast, he felt that he had, indeed, banqueted, and that he could now, like the Tartar khan after his repast on the sumptuous horse-flesh and mare's milk, flourish the trumpet and proclaim that all the rest of the world could go now to grub.

Almost as quickly as the shifting of a gypsy encampment scene from the stage, in a drama, our canvas domicile and the paraphernalia of the camp were transposed from the woodland to the canoe. Blackened logs half burned, charred chunks, heaps of ashes, strips of birch bark, a mixed rubbish of trout heads, fins and skeletons, potato skins, a drift of hemlock boughs, scraps of paper, lithographed tobacco labels, and other minor refuse, were all the vestiges left to testify of our recent homestead.

About eight o'clock we tucked ourselves in the canoe, and, without much ado, bade a somewhat regretful adieu to Chickabiddy Camp. The christening of the spot with that name was a chance freak of caprice merely, but a memory of the place and of our four days' life there will survive long in the future of our several recollections. A half-mile below it, we saw a handsome fawn, with its coat of many spots, standing fixed and still at the mouth of a petty rill. It certainly did not have its eye-teeth cut, or it would not have stood there, within range, a tempting mark for a deadly shot. But we were abreast of it, or slightly below, when it was discovered, and before Thebault had fumbled his pocket and found a cap and got the rifle well in hand, the rapid current had swept us furtherward, and distance had made it safe. The crack of the gun sent the startled fawn bounding, but unharmed, out of sight.

There had been so much trout and so great deficit of deer since we left the Michigami, that such a sight brought imaginary flavors of venison to our lips, and we longed for a real haunch. While our birch was sliding easily along, and our thoughts were yet, possibly, brooding over the evanescent fawn, Thebault, the far-seer, discerned and pointed to us another statuesque object, a large-horned buck, cooling himself in the stream, and there

> "With his imperial front,
> Shaggy and bold, and wreathed horns superb,
> The breathing creature stood."

He was too far for Thebault's rifle, and caught sight of us too soon to admit of any stealth or strategy being played on him by the rifleman. Still,

Thebault determined to give him a scare. When the deer turned for the bushes, the gun was shot, and the terrorized buck plunged and tore the water wide open in his panic haste to set his hoofs on shore.

On the advance, the rods were plied in such reaches, below such rapids, and behind such rock or boulder masses, as promised immediate results; and these brief snatches of angling were sufficient to furnish us an ample dinner and supper supply. In these passings, which were nearing us to the mouth of the river, we scarcely recognized the Brulé we voyaged formerly. Then, a primitive density of forest bordered, and unbroken solitude brooded over the shores to the very mouth. Since then, the logman's axe has been diligent in clearing spaces in the wood, and the massive foliage that crowned the close towering pines, in whose shadows and silence the river of trout ran undisturbed, remote from busy haunts of men, has, in several places, disappeared, and vistas stretch into the depths and to the verge of the sky. These clearings leave a rugged and stumpy appearance, and strip the ground of the glorious livery of verdure that robed and hid its barrenness and poverty. These places are now occasional, at least, in the lower ten miles, and, to us, changed the old landmarks.

But we struck one familiar point when we put in to Camp Thebault for dinner. It and its environs were unchanged. There were wildness and forest enough of virginal nature to make it a fitting range for the wolf, whose howl we had there heard in the distance. When there before, we had imprinted, with a Faber, on a large pine, fresh barked for the purpose, our names and the figures of the catch. Recalling the "trivial fond records" of previous troutings by other parties, as we had found them inscribed on trees, we then supposed we were leaving behind us a proud triumphal memorial of angling prowess, by scoring, in emphatic prominence, the figures of seven hundred and seventy-four.

Looking now at these, our own figures of before, we thought we could put on airs—certainly over our former selves—and lay rather flattering unction to our souls, in view of the statistical results of this trip. It counted a total of thirteen hundred and eighty-eight. The individual figures, or those of each in this total, ranked High considerably first, Pratt next, myself third, and, because of his earlier return, Denison last, in the rivalry and credit of exploits with the rod. A more imposing maximum might easily have been reached with only a few more daily hours spent in the effort. The few scores of a single catching fully satisfied the demands of a reasonable sporting ambition for the time, while other possible scores would have been wanton and wasteful excess. A superfluity palled the keenness of appetite. The smaller fry we invariably returned to the water.

When at dinner, and as he prodded his fifth trout with his fork, High remarked that he had always heard and thought that blessings brighten as they take their flight, and in view of the imminent vanishment of the luscious trout meals, he intended to make the most of the last to be set before him. After so long breakfasting, dining, supping and sleeping on trout, this certainly showed a healthy and still appreciatory appetence for trout. We all agreed in applying Dr. Butler's praise of the strawberry to trout: "Doubtless God might have made a better fish, but doubtless God never did." However, for my own part, I owned up to a trifle of satiety on trout, and it would be no serious gastronomic penance to me to take leave of that daintiest dish until the next or other season's excursion.

At all events, the trouting was practically ended. The lines were wound up, the reels were rubbed dry and wrapped, the rods were slid into their final covers, and the baskets were stuffed with odds and ends. The fishing campaign, we knew, was over, as we swept into sight of a lumberman's cabin a mile above the mouth of the Brulé, in a clearing cut out since our former knowledge of the river. It was of the usual style of the logman's quarters —a parallelogram of pine logs, low and long, and roofed with shakes, fitted with bunks for sleeping, and with a center board table for meals. It is the winter quarters of the hardy cutters whose axes level the forest and convert it into logs to be floated on the spring freshets to the mills, whence, as lumber, the pine is dispersed over wide regions.

To this cabin we designed a visitation, and hove to at the landing place. We knew by a pale, bluish film of smoke rising above the roof that some living soul was on the premises. To our knock responded a man and a dog. It was a response of welcome from both. It was easy to see in the shiny, oily face of the man, in his costume glossed with grease, and from his odor redolent of kitchen pots and dishwater, that he was the cook. He was short, pursy and bald; a French-Canadian, and was not wanting in the reputed affability of his race. As only three or four men were now of his household, his duties were not pressing, and he had leisure to smoke his well-blackened brier-wood pipe and lazily parley with us.

We were welcome to any supplies we might require, and as replenishment of the larder was the chief purpose of the visit, he supplied our necessities of pork, flour, potatoes and tobacco, as well as spared us a Chicago Sunday newspaper a fortnight old. Bobbie, his dog, was not less sociable, and when we patted him, wagged us his tail in friendly welcome, and hospitably rubbed his nose on our trousers. Parts of the walls were a rude art gallery, formed of wood-cuts, clippings from pictorial papers and police gazettes far out of date, cheap, flaming, high-colored lithographs, and for a devotional subject, an engraving of saint and saintess in flamboyant robes. These, and familiar kitchen and household appliances, reminded us that we were now approaching the regions of settlement, the frontier of civilization.

It was curious to recall, that since we left Republic, until we faced this sylvan pot-slinger, and with the exception of the redskin and the squaws on the Paint, we had not seen a human face or habitation, or signs of them, unless the trails we trod over may be considered such signs. The portages are so seldom imprinted by a human foot, that nature almost reclaims them, by growths and fallen timber, back to their natural wildness, so that they are often obscure and treacherous. A travel by land and water, as long and as far as ours, and through regions as wide apart, with nothing in sight but all-pervading nature, and not even a single token of man's presence, serves to show the utter silence, vastness and wildness of the wilderness, still primitive in the forms impressed by the Creator. He alone was present on the noiseless and solitary pathways of our advance.

The summer livery of the forests will have many a season to decay and grow again, and again to fade and fall, before much of this great wilderness shall blossom as the rose. And we were then not out of the woods. This was about the last of the Brulé, for a mile below the logging cabin it and the Paint commingle their waters, and, flowing together five or six miles, the Michigami adds its volume, and the blended affluents become the Menominee. We portaged ourselves over the rough trail from above and around the Brulé falls, while the Indians shot the birch-bark, bounding like a cork among the dangerous boulders, and through the tossing breakers of the rapids, safely and quickly into still water. We had time, while the traps were being borne over the carry, to read the legends on the trees, which are numerous in figures and names. Among those surviving "decay's effacing fingers," we found our own former memorials done in Bissell's boldest autographic scrawl. To these was now added a supplementary inscription of the present party. Many of these rude tablets of the trees were curious and eccentric in their chirography and spelling, and some of them were in a jingle of rhyme. It would seem that usually, Brulé troutsmen were not wearied with an affluence of sport.

The goal of the day's voyaging was Badwater, and Tom King's cabin there. We had enthusiastically invited ourselves to be his guests, and to give him a friendly surprise. We foretold ourselves a cordial reception. Our time-table was so set that we and the night would come together at that point. But the day advanced more fleetly than our canoe.

We could not go down as fast as the evening sun declined. The paddles strained a point in the way of propulsive effort, and sped the craft gallantly on, and though she sprang like a spurred courser ahead, it was evident, when we saw the sunset reddening already into rosy flush, and we were yet some miles off, the propelling machinery would be unequal to the task. So the Indians slowed the advance, and, a couple of miles below the confluence of the Michigami and the other mingled streams, where the Menominee debouches into several channels, forming little islands, we turned ashore to encamp. It was at a point where these several branches join the main river, and we could command a view of the silvery threads of stream.

On the inside of the point there was a huge log-drift lodged and heaved up by the freshets. Trunks of all sized trees were swept into a shapeless jam and jagged chaos. The top ledge of this massive interwedged drift was at least thirty feet above the water-mark, showing the height and force of the floods that had whirled them there. There was a glut of fuel, and we had no trouble, with the lurid irradiation of the heaping camp-fire, in driving back the deep shadows of the night.

In the morning the bones of the last trout mess were left strewn around the breakfast log. Our trout-pampered epicurism was now ended. With the exception of the prospective venison from expected deer further down, our repasts in the future voyaging would be reduced to the staples of cookery. It is said that kingfishers encase their nests in the banks with a lining of fish-bones. Our encampments on the Brulé must have proved windfalls of trout skeletonry to the kingfishers there, and if the kingfishers, so many of which made our acquaintance, lined their nests with our leavings, our wanderings and sojournings must have been a happy godsend to them. This allusion was suggested by a kingfisher which, near to us, swooped down and dipped his plumage for an unwary sucker or chub as a breakfast meal.

The anticipated sensation of the day was our intended and self-invited call on our former Menominee guide, Tom King, of Badwater. His pagan name is *Weawbiny-Ket*. Our Menominees interpreted it as *Weawbiny*, white, and *Ket*, arm. So his native alias means White-arm. Literally, on account of his dark coppery complexion, the expression is incongruous and a misnomer. But we chose to take it as meaning whiteness in the figurative sense of quality; as when it is said of a man that he is white, and, in that liberal interpretative spirit we were contemplating a reception worthy of a man and a brother. It was our cue to descend on him as a surprise party, and I intended taking, as is not unusual in such fashionable and impromptu invasions, refreshments of a cheering and festive kind.

So as we neared Badwater and swung into the reach where his cabin was visible, and knew from the blue smoke which thinly curled up from the chimney that somebody was at home, the paddles dipped quicker strokes to speed us to the place.

Nobody, however, appeared to hail our coming. In fact, as we drew up at the landing place, the open door of the mansion was promptly shut with an emphatic slam. We failed to observe any latch string hanging out. Neither squaw, papoose or Weawbiny-ket even yet appeared with an eye to mark our coming and grow brighter as we came. In truth, the surprise party was a surprised party. When our surprise gave way to reflection, we concluded that sort of thing was Indian style, for the similarly meaning formula of good society, not at home. However, we thought we would not be too sensitive, or put too fine a point on it. We were in serious need of pitch to smear the canoe, and like Falstaff, hiding our honor in our necessity, we dispatched Thebault, as bearer of dispatches, on a mission of inquiry to Madame King, the Weawbiny-kettle of the domicile. He met the matron at the doorway, and held a threshold pow-wow with her.

As the result of his embassage, our envoy informed us that Tom himself was absent up the Michigami, and further, that Denison and Pratt had invaded her premises, at midnight, during a rain storm, drenched and in a high state of appetite. This circumstance enlightened us, and was probably the key to the mystery of the Weawbiny-kettle cold shoulder shown us. Those famished and inundated gentlemen had possibly laid waste all the provisions in the house, as well as moistly monopolized the family beds and blankets, and sent the mother squaw and the little Weawbiny-kittens to the kitchen floor to worry away a hapless night. Possibly, therefore, a second apparition of pale faces, just from the woods, reduced to meagre rations, was a symbol to her untutored mind of famine and freezing both. Giving the accused the benefit of the doubt, then, we wrapped ourselves in our imaginary mantles of charity, and, in a benignant frame of mind, we were prepared to go on our way, forgiving and forgetting our metaphorical and vicarious slap in the face on account of Denison and Pratt.

We ran across the river, and advanced, in full force, to a cabin there, for a supply of pitch. We found there one intimidated squaw and three papooses, "one little, two little, three little Indian boys." But as to the pitch, there was not to be had enough to verify the proverb that whoever toucheth pitch he is defiled. We left Badwater with our colors at half-mast, so to speak. Two miles below was Badwater Crossing, a ferry established the previous year for the road to the logging camp near Brulé falls. This road marks an inroad of civilization, and pioneers the advance of man into the domain of nature.

At the crossing is a pine-log cabin, with pretensions to be classed as an inn, judging from the legend "Montreal Badwater House," imprinted on a splint or shake over the main door. It stands on a high smooth bluff, in a handsome situation, at the convex point of a curve in the river. It has several apartments. There was a garden with familiar potato vines, beets and cabbage. Paul Miller is the Boniface, and because there was a bright-eyed, comely woman to mistress it, the household was all snug, neat and tidy, and had an appearance of home comfort. To support its tavernous pretensions, it had just had at least one guest named on its register. That was D. H. Lloyd, of the Chicago Tribune, who had a few days sojourned there. After satisfying a modest ambition with his rifle in tapping a deer's blood and securing the carcass to be sent to the city, he had undauntedly set out on the home return, on a stout pair of shanks, through the woods to a point on the new railroad. He had stored here a gem of a birch-bark canoe, nearly tiny, pretty and light enough for a fairy craft—not much larger than a Manitoba snow-shoe, and fitted only for a crew of one.

Here we found a package of Chicago journals, and letters from those who had something sweet and domestic to tell of home, forwarded by Arthur

T. Jones, of Marinette. We appreciated the civility and attention of this gentleman. He is himself a devoted and skillful brother of the angle, and is one of those of whom it is said, in the words of the milkmaid's mother, in the Complete Angler: "All anglers be such honest, civil, quiet men." For his kindness to us we would wish fortune to "set him in a shower of gold, and hail rich pearls upon him."

Yet papers and letters only momentarily diverted our thoughts, but did not inspire longings for the homes and the world beyond, whose messages and news they bore us. We were still so much in spirit with our surroundings that neither Gibbon's fight, nor Hall's discovery of a satellite of Mars, nor the war of Osmanli and Muscovite, nor the perturbations of finance, nor any freshet of news could then sensationalize us out of the charm, composure and *dolce far niente* of our uncompleted voyage. We would foretaste or borrow no sensations. We would be soon enough returned to the fret and friction of city and business life. We wanted our drift into activity at high pressure to be as smooth, quiet and gentle as the flow of the river. So our newspapers hardly rippled, for the moment, the ease and calm of the way, and of our way of life. The hours were golden with us, but we were not fain to chase them with flying feet. Passing each of the cascades of the Twin falls, we sidled ashore at a curving ledge of rock rising up to an elevation. Its face was thinly streaked with a shag or scanty nap of moss, and up the side was clothed with a thicket of stunted trees, in the shade of which we were served to good purpose, with some of Paul Miller's contributions to the larder. Just below there were some ugly rapids with wildly pitching billows. It seemed that one's time had possibly come should he dare a passage, which for the canoe was clearly an extra-hazardous risk which a prudent underwriter would not insure against to the value of a pin's fee. The natives checked up on the verge of the turbulence, and took circumspective glances, and parleyed a little and pondered more. We knew the venture was a dubious one. The nervous organizations of Chicago, at least, were not absolutely placid.

I noticed that on close approach to the "vex'd Bermoothes," High lifted his eyes from a highly seasoned Milwaukee divorce scandal and family racket in a newspaper, with the details of which he had been engrossed, and devoted his particular solicitude to the raging breakers. I shared his anxiety, and thought "If it were done, then t'were well it were done quickly." But the Indians at length unleashed the craft and let it loose. It bounded among heaving waters rushingly. The reckless white-caps, like enraged and frantic water sprites, with mad foam frothing their lips, tossed and leaped up to us as if they would board the birch-bark, and lap us in their watery embrace. We shot through the seething peril very rapidly, however, with no mishap more serious than a few splashes, and scooping in two or three of the more daring white-caps. High resumed the perusal of the matrimonial sensation of Milwaukee.

The few miles to Big Quiniseck Falls were miles of uniformly beautiful scenery. In some reaches the stream glided partly under the shade of the forest, and then on curving around a bend spread into full radiance of the sun, so that we were flitting from light to shade; but the river was placid as a painted meadow brook. The stillness of the entire scene was impressive: not a leaf trembling to the sigh of a breeze, not a twig moving, not air enough astir to breathe a film of agitation; only the widening ripples cut by the canoe and the spirals from the dip of the paddles, to mar the mirror-like gloss and calm of the stream, and like silence of the bordering woods, with scarce a note or chirp or twitter of a bird: this was a stillness which could hardly be found elsewhere. We insensibly assimilated ourselves in spirit to the profound and all-pervading calm, and sympathetically lapsed into a serenity and langour in harmony with the overpowering hush and repose of nature. Dreamily, passively, voicelessly and restfully, we kept in this luxurious drowse of enchantment till we neared Big Quiniseck Falls. Only the rumble of the falling waters broke the charm.

We had scarcely recovered from the spell before our birch bark touched the head of the trail. The portage is a wearisome trudge of two miles, a pathway for single-filing, and almost smothered in the profusion of bushes, which often tripped the feet or switched in our faces. High and I shouldered the blanket packs and led off, and with much weariness of flesh and in copious sweat of the brow, slowly paced the seemingly interminable, and occasionally almost impenetrable route. Ours, though, was a trifling labor compared with the task of Thebault and Paul. They twice plodded over the route, and even their stalwart frames weakened and tired under the strain; and before the carry was all finished, and they had borne the canoe through the sea of foliage, the twilight overspread us in its gathered shades.

We tented on the high point of rock on the Michigan side. We had a commanding view of the scenery, striking yet, though sobered into dimmer outline. But in the glow of the morning sun the scenery was beautiful exceedingly. At our feet the foam from the cataract washed the edge of the shore, and laid in streaks like drifts of snow. The currents in the eddies curved gracefully, bearing flakes and tufts of foam. Just by, the misty spray rose like a phantom drapery of silvery smoke over the rushing waters of the falls. The perspective down the river was not less charming.

In fact, the whole scenery of these falls, the wildness and beauty, the forest and stream, need only the genius of some Claude Lorraine, Turner or Church to trace and color them in the immortal glories of art, to make them world-known and famed and sought. Some day, tourists in search of the picturesque and artists in pursuit of studies, will come out of their way to take in Big Quiniseck Falls. Pictures of them in the memory of the one, and on the canvass of the other, would well match, or surpass, those of many a view more famed of art and story. These were the impressions of the former trip, and now they were more than renewed.

# CHAPTER XIX.

A SPORTSMAN'S CAMP — AMENITIES OF THE WOODS — LITTLE QUINISECK FALLS—SAND RAPID—STURGEON FARM—A HAT—STURGEON FALLS—DR. ANDREWS—PEEMBINWUN RAPIDS—A PICKEREL INCIDENT—INDIAN ENCAMPMENT—PEEMONY FALLS—RIVER SCENES.

AFTER starting, not many minutes of paddling brought within view, in the distance, a scene of quite another sort, which put an end to our impressions of the grand and beautiful, and set our emotions to quite another key. A couple of tents on the bank, in white relief against a deep emerald background, with figures standing or moving about, proclaimed a camp. Nearing more closely, we knew by the token of a deer-skin stretched to dry, and from the red-shirted Indians, and a group of men in hunting coats in the foreground, that we had come upon a sportsman's encampment. When within hail, we were saluted with a hearty "Good morning, gentlemen, won't you land?" There was a very generous alacrity on our part to accept the invitation, and we promptly turned in and laid alongside the pine-log pier and disembarked.

There were no preliminary formalities. The shaken hands at once endenizened us, as it were, in the full freedom of the camp, and the pledge or ceremony of investiture with such freedom was a a pipe apiece to smoke, and a cup of kindness from the confidential demijohn. These hospitalities were agreeably improved by us. We exchanged short and rapid expeditionary histories. Our friends, as we felt them to be, were a Chicago party, at the head of which was Robert Clark, the well-known veteran woods sportsman, with Ira Augur, W. B. Wilcox, and C. E. Fargo, as his fellows. They had five Chippewa camp followers, luggers and polers.

They had journeyed overland, and three days previously struck the river and set up their canvass quarters at this point. The canoe flotilla and the Indians had come on in advance and to await them. They had already had a prelude of gunning and game, and had shot and feasted on two deer; of one of these they spared us an acceptable haunch with their compliments, and with gratefulness from us. They were well equipped for all the contingencies; and were bound for the Brulé. Our brief meeting with them was a delightful episode of socialities and kindnesses on surprise, and an instance of the rough and spontaneous friendliness of the woods. We heartily wished them *bon voyage*, and gave them our friendliest adieus.

Little Quiniseck Falls are not now as grand as we saw them in their primitive and natural estate. Science, capital and labor have shorn them of much of their natural grandeur. Some combined lumber companies are waging a strife against nature for their improvement. The design is to merge the separate runs of water into one, which is to be freed, by blasting, from the rocks that formerly split or broke in pieces the logs pitching over. By a temporary wing-dam, the water is forced into the Wisconsin chute, while the Michigan branch is having its rock blasted out piecemeal, and huge masses and ledges of the granite were being blown from foundations as old and firm as those of the everlasting hills.

Man with capital, and giant powder as his dynamic agent, will soon prevail, and cataracts that for ages have been untamed and unchanged, will be made obedient and pliant servitors to his needs. When the one channel is excavated or blasted out, and the whole river turned into it, there will be little of the natural grandeur of the cascade left. When we passed there, we found an encampment of many men who were working the drills and blasts. Powder and steel have wrought wonders, but these wonders of skill and science have nearly effaced some of the impressive wonders of nature. In the basin below, where I had formerly but vainly dropped in hook and line, one of the brawny drill-pickers had been bobbing for fish, and had nipped nearly a score of bass and wall-eyed pike.

Preparatory to attempting the Sand Rapid we lunched, not far below the falls, on a rocky point. These rapids are an ordeal of peril to the frail birch-barks. They are three miles of boulders, breakers, shallows, whirls and dashes, in one stretch. The trail around is two miles, and zig-zags up a spur of elevation—quite the most considerable up-hill elevation of the route yet passed—and strained our pedestrianism to its utmost. On the plateau was a sparseness of forest in places, there were woods elsewhere with prostrate trees over which we climbed and scrambled through the branches, with much peril to the rods we carried. On the other and descending side of the hill-spur, the trail was lost in grasses and bushes, and down on the level, the tangle of fallen timber and undergrowth was such that we thought the way hopelessly barred and lost.

We aimlessly struggled through the obstructive maze, without a visible trace of the path, and sinking at every step in the plashes of the marsh. By accident, we came upon a dragway for logs, which we followed up, and it led us to the river. By clambering and balancing on treacherous trunks in the log-drifts, and jumping from stone to stone, in the edge of the water, and by scuffling through thickets, we finally made our way, exhausted, to the foot of the Rapid.

This was just in time to see the Dickey heave in sight, the paddles swinging briskly from side to side, winding with the coiling channel, sometimes checked and eased up with the poles, then shooting ahead in bounding swiftness, and nearing us, rounding and gracefully riding in the still water at our feet. We thankfully blessed the good fortune that, through the dangerous passing, she was

"Held up so tenderly,
Fashioned so slenderly,"

as to come in unharmed in perfect trim.

We ran near a woodchuck swimming across. We veered a bit one side, so Thebault could jab his head under water with the paddle. The submersion only enraged the creature. He emerged, snorting the water from his nostrils, and spunkily turned and swam toward us in our wake, as if to fight the whole party, spitting viciously at us like a mad cat. His pluck was appreciated. We declined the skirmish. We preferred to give him our benediction. We let him go, with the magnanimous words of Uncle Toby to the fly, "Go, poor devil; the world is large enough for us all."

The next port of entry was the New York farm, at the mouth of Sturgeon river. As our carrying capacity was less than our consuming ability, the robustness of our forest-sharpened appetite brought us frequently to the verge of depletion, and now the viands were running short again. It was necessary to victual the expedition; we therefore landed in a stress of pork and tubers. I was deputed to attend to this commercial, or rather commissariat business. Thebault, bearing bag and basket, attended me as master of transportation. As a provisional deputation we climbed the sandy path up the steep bank, and presently interviewed the business man of the demesne. The figures on his price current were reasonable, the supplies abundant, and the traffic was completed before our heels had time to cool.

During the interval of the chaffering, the ladies of the family or household strewed the full-blown roses of their smiles on our path, and to us who had been fellows so long to the weeds, herbage and other vestures of the wilderness, such flowers were winsomely sweet and pleasant—"too pleasant to be looked upon except on holidays"—and they made a brief holiday to us. The grangeresses or patronesses of husbandry, it is true, very curiously eyed my hat askance, as though they were sure that they never saw anything quite like that head-gear. Still I hoped I had acquitted myself in the way of civility and *devoirs* quite as well as High did at the Wausauka tents, when the ladies giggled at him in his gallant role of Turveydrop.

In fact the hat was something phenomenal. Its original linen dome-shape was speckled like a guinea-hen, and from its resemblance to the spotted plumage of that barn-yard fowl, Denison nicknamed the chapeau guinea-hen, and I was not critical enough nicely to consider whether that name was a misnomer. The hat had been presented to me expressly for the trip; by a near relative of an ex-president of the United States, and as this was nearest to anything in the way of executive patronage I ever received, I felt bound to make the most of the gift. It had an indestructibility equal to that of a nine-lived cat. It had been trampled on, sat on, slept on, rained on, shined on, dried in the sun, shrivelled by the fire, turned inside out, with its brim looped up and also flapped down, and had moulded itself into most varied shapes, and still retained the essential utilities of a hat. It entirely eclipsed my felt hat.

We had news of Denison and Pratt at this place; they had put in there under stress of circumstances, and had been compelled to abandon and condemn the Tom King as unseaworthy, probably from her having been rough-used and battered in the labyrinths of the Sand Rapid. Fortunately, they relieved themselves from their stranded condition by being able to get teamed, from the farm, a few miles to the new railroad for a train.

From the farm to Sturgeon Falls is a mile; over a high back-bone of a hill, the trail winds to the foot of the cascade; short as the portage was, it was panting work to climb it. Lowering clouds obscured the setting sun, and tokened the quick advance of showers from the west; we hasted to set our house in order, and had but barely reared the canopy, when the skirmish line of the charging clouds opened on us and nearly beat out the campfire, and forced us into shelter. Supper was served in the tent by the feeble glimmering of the fitful tallow-dip. Soon the heavier and massed squadrons of rain-clouds swept over, and delivered us rain in torrents; there was thunder resonance, with flashings of lightning.

It was a scene of great moisture; drops trickled through some pores of the tent, and our inner atmosphere was grievously humid; the supply of hemlock boughs, for embedding on, was scant; the dreams of broken sleep, the beating of the rain and the dampness made it a night of dismal phantasmagoria to us. The morn did not come in russet mantle clad. Though the heaviest of the storm had passed, a train or rear-guard of scowling clouds hung back portentously looming. On a memorial tree we saw inscribed the names of Doctor E. Andrews and sons, of Chicago, who had encamped here the previous night. We were prompt, as soon as we had breakfasted and stowed the cargo, to start on our way rejoicing from the forbidding spot.

At the strip of shore where Pratt had, on the

previous trip killed a fawn, fresh deer-tracks imprinted the sand. He had then declared perpetual truce and amity with the deer kind. But Thebault was not so compunctious or tender-hearted, and was on the lookout for the hoofed and antlered "native burghers of the desert city." It was life and liberty to those recent deer that they had seasonably made tracks out of the way, which was all we saw of them. Clark's venison had now gone the way of all flesh of the haunch, that is to pot, and we depended for fresh meat on the rifle. We were, therefore, advancing in a state of armed reconnoisance.

At Peembinwun rapids the Menominee was almost shrunken literally to bed-rock. The whole loading was put ashore and carried around. The canoe was safely, though at hazard of wrecking, guided through. There was a fine vesture of grass in the shade, and we had lunch there, and reclining on the grass, we leisurely sipped the Oolong tea procured at Sturgeon farm, and much at ease enjoyed the prandial snack. Three Chippewas, on the way above for deer, stopped for portaging their canoes and for rest, at this point. They and our natives held a brief international or intertribal council on the ground, in one of their maternal tongues. It was not encouraging to our aspirations or rather stomach for venison, expected below, that these redskins had left from below, and were out to peer the country over our just traversed course, in deer-slaying cohoot.

There was a pickerel entertainment here, also. Just off our canoe, at the beach, High espied a large pickerel, about two feet in length, sunning himself or sleeping in shoal water. On account of my tourney with one of the same species at Michigami falls, High pointed him to me as the pickerel champion. But I declined the exertion of unsheathing, jointing up and rigging my rod for even so promising a diversion. Thereupon, Thebault attempted to knock out the fish's brains with the pushing pole, but the pickerel dodged, and bore off his brains with him to the deeper water. But presently, the officious fish swam again into sight. This hardihood now roused High's piscatory blood; but how to harmonize it and his piscatory taste, to which baiting seemed only foul play and wholly repugnant, was a perplexity—for a moment. He knew a pickerel would turn up its nose at a fly gewgaw. So, to compromise himself only partially, he tacked on what we supposed was a slit of bacon with a new glaring red-fly.

High clambered to a rock in reach of the fish, and gently swung in the gorgeous mongrel scarecrow right by the fish's snout. As was to be expected, the monstrous thing-of-a-jig terrified the pickerel into fits, and it shot off like a flash into the deep. Such an egregious *fiasco* would set any table in a roar, and the jest was too much for even Indian gravity. High manfully bore our broad grins, but when he was chaffed for baiting with ignominious pork, he vehemently resented the derogatory imputation, and protested it was a tittle of deer grafted on the fly. We had not been aware that there was a venison fibre on hand, and though, in his word, I generally considered him, like Horatio, "as just a man as e'er my conversation cop'd withal," I was after all sceptical about the deer.

Not far below was an encampment of Indians, squaws, papooses and dogs, who had come up from White Rapids for a sojourn in bark tepees, on a general shooting and curing of deer for winter. One of the men had just punctured a buck, though not so mortally but that the shot animal was able to get away with his antlers and the bullet into unknown parts of Michigan. As we came along, the savage was squatted in his canoe, musing like a sage how receding deer, like other blessings, are most prized when they take their flight. The pickerel exploit inspired High with a fellow feeling that made him look wondrous kind and sympathetic toward the discomfited copper-skin.

On the Peemony Falls portage, a handsome trail, we failed to find any of the blueberries which, on the former occasion, so plentifully bespangled the ground, like dewdrops in blue. Just below there is a cultivated farm, with the most pretentious habitation on the river, having an existing household and home, and it is really the most advanced outpost of agriculture on the river. On the bank below it, an hour's run, were two clearings or meadows, with Indian cabins. At one of them, a couple of youthful Chippewas, in primitive duds and innocence, stood on the bank and curiously gazed at us passing, as if we were an unaccustomed apparition. Three miles further down was one of our former camping grounds. The shadows of evening that were gathering, as well as considerations of kettle and pan, joined in directing and hastening us there as an encampment for the night.

The hand of innovation had made notable changes; the forest that shadowed the river, had been thinned out, and the landmarks were difficult of recognition; though, on the opposite shore, the dense wood still reared up, in its native wildness, its dark and solemn outlines. These more frequent clearings and deadenings have destroyed much of the beauty of the lower Menominee scenery; the many leafless trees, gaunt, stripped, blackened by fire, or dead from girdling, in the garish sun, give a forlorn and naked appearance. The denuded land, however, after being stripped of its timber, converted into logs and floated to the mills, is left barren and unpeopled, and is not sown for harvests or cultivated for homes and habitations. The charms of voyaging the stream are rapidly vanishing;

while the luxuriance of nature is being shorn away, it is not replaced with the tokens and evidences of life and labor.

These occasional disafforested strips, which have made unsightly gaps in the massiveness of the woods, present an appearance of utter waste or desert, strangely at variance with the luxuriant density of the wilderness elsewhere. The growths of weeds and stunted shrubbery that creep over the ground, unpleasantly mark both the despoliation of the original forest wealth and the sterility or poverty of the soil itself. It will probably be very many years before the smoke of domestic altars in cottagers' abodes will ascend in these clearings, as signs of farm or pastoral life, and of homes of contented labor and enterprise and prospective wealth.

## CHAPTER XX.

WHITE RAPIDS—TROUT BROOKLET—PIKE RIVER AND WANI-TAH—SIXTY ISLANDS—YELLOW DOGS—RAVENS—HIGH AS PADDLER—JIM KAQUOTASH—LONE PINE CAMP—EVENING SCENE—LOWER MENOMINEE—DOCTOR ANDREWS—THE END—ST. PETER'S BLESSING.

It was not a long paddle we had of it to White Rapids. High and I took to the pathway through the meadow-like stretch of ground, thinly fringed on the bank with small trees, casting a meagre ragged shade, and left the Indians to work the canoe through the shoals and rapids. The trouting fever showed symptoms on High as soon as we touched the trail. He recalled his reminiscences of the rather difficult, but not unpleasant sport before, at the brooklet. It was easy to presage his wishes from the tone of his recollections, and from his solicitude about the signs of the weather, of which he took constant observations from the clouds.

Before the fever had risen to its climacteric, the

sky was more ominous of a shower, and, even his enthusiasm for a trial of the fly, among clumps of bushes and thickets of alder, oozed away on account of the probable moisture of the attempt. He admitted it would hardly pay to wet his jacket for the trout, and thought it preferable to take the chances of rain with the tent at hand to be landed for ready shelter. Though, as this was the last known possibility of trout on the nearly ended trip, he wavered and faltered in will and purpose till we depossibleized the venture by getting him actually embarked and under way.

At the mouth of Pike river, the pine-wood bower or boudoir of the dusky Indian maid and kennel of the Cerberus dog were shut up and deserted. Paul was a trifle emotional on this occasion, possibly expecting to have had a brief scene of eyes looking love to eyes that would speak again, or something to that effect. The young buck heaved a bit of a sigh as we went skipping by. We passed the Sixty Islands. These are an archipelago of islands and islets, a cluster of glorious emerald, of various forms and sizes, with splendid profusely branched and leaved elms, a very wealth of verdure, making a view of the most lovely and picturesque scenery.

We were content to float, at times, on the current rather than outspeed it with strokes of the paddles, that we might lingeringly enjoy the surpassing beauty. From a cabin we were passing, a yellow dog ran out and followed on the bank, barking at us savagely, making the welkin ring with his howls, until he yelped all the wind out of him. High was facetious enough to hint that guineahen hat as the cause of the yellow whelp's convulsions. Down further, Thebault fired the rifle at a plover that was strutting about wetting its toes in the edge of the river. The charge had been loaded, far above, for expected deer. They were frequent on our first descent of this river. On this voyage, excepting the two near Camp Chickabiddy, we had not seen one of the "dappled fools." The railroad to the Breen mines, the clearings and the many stranded logs along shore, were said by an Indian hunter, to frighten them from the river.

By the side of a couple of canoes drawn up in the grass, was another Yellow Dog, with a comrade. This was quite a different sort of a yellow dog from the ill-begotten cur that had shown his teeth to us—no other than a well-known old Indian of that name, of Twin Island habitancy. Thebault and Paul well knew him. They held up, and he and his dilapidated chum and themselves fired volleys of Indian gab promiscuously and interchangeably. He must have been a witty dog, for his sallies generally brought down our men in rather boisterous merriment. Doctor Andrews' party was reported by them to have passed down shortly before. I am not enough versed in the theory of omens to judge whether the croakings of a funereal party of ravens, perched on a dead tree near the river, which we heard, were sepulchral forebodings or monitions of mortality instinctively excited by the appearance of a doctor to their prophetic eyes.

By noon we were at Wausauka bend. Instead of doubling the long narrow promontory on the water, we trod the portage across its base. We intended dining there. When we camped there before, we were swarmed on by the most multitudinous and ravenous mosquitoes of the whole journey. And now, no sooner were our packs laid down, than flying legions of the blood-thirsty fiends encompassed us round about. Among the leaders of the winged lancers, we recognized that demon vampyre of the gory host and of his species, the gallinipper. The onset was too much for us, and the demoralized party fled the field and rallied on a further point.

We went through the Long Reach, which is a beautiful, straight and wide perspective of river scenery. Instead of having his esthetic sensibilities moved, as an impressionable voyager would, by such blended charms of wood and stream, High was seized with a sudden dementia or idiosyncrasy of propulsion. He grasped Thebault's paddle, and with it enthusiastically buffeted the water, wielding it rapidly, like an orchestra leader swaying his baton in allegro passages of the score. The canoe, under his vigorous impulsion, jerked ahead in gallant style.

His mode of paddling, though, was rather exhaustive and·not likely to be long-winded. He bended forward to plunge the paddle up to the handle, and then throwing himself back, swung a deep, long back stroke, making the water swirl, and "in convolution swift the feathered eddy float," when he lifted out the blade at the end of the sweep. The eccentricity of performance that most concerned me was, however, the over-shifting of the paddle from one to the other side. It scattered the drip from it over me as if from a shower-bath, and with copious dampening effects on the cargo, to say nothing of the danger of my crown being banged by some of its wayward motions. His lunacy of paddling, though exciting solicitude, was amusing. It tickled Thebault and Paul more than his pickerel experiment with the red fly and equivocal venison. However we could all see that, with the necessary practice, High has a great future before him as a paddler. But a mile of this health-lift took the wind out of him.

Just above the Relay House rapids, there was an Indian's castle of bark. The family linen hung out to dry. This was a token, if not of so much cleanliness as is next to godliness, at least of the red inmates having reached the saponaceous stage of civilization. A copper-sheathed Stentor on shore hailed our boys in a tone loud enough for a camp-meeting preacher. Their reply was *sotto voce* comparatively. But they held a parley in tongues unknown to us. It appeared that the stentorian aborigine was Jim Kaquotash, a brother of our auxiliary Kaquotashes. He told of a *weawbiny* man who had passed down but little in advance of us. This we knew to be Dr. Andrews. We hoped to run him down and to extend to him the hospitalities of our camp for the night, or, if his hospitalities were more liberal than ours, that is, if his cornucopia was less impoverished than our cornucopia, to permit ourselves to be invited to go snacks with him. But the Grand Rapids separated us. We navigated them safely, but slowly, and in doing so grazed low submerged rocks, rubbed on stones, cut through breakers and sometimes stuck on flats.

The last camp of the former trip, at Twin Island, the poor demesne of Yellow Dog, was a wretched one, with torrents of rain, and the mosquitoes of all out-of-doors. But the last camp of this trip was attended with all the charm of our roughing and tenting all the way round about. It was on a high bank of clearing, a sward smooth and handsome as a lawn ; not far over on the other side was a fine alluvial natural meadow; overshadowing the tent, a splended, solitary pine tree, doubtless spared from the axe for its stateliness. From this, we named our encampment Lone Pine Camp.

The air was soft, pure and balmy. When twilight deepened into dark, we stretched on the grass, on the brink of the river, and watched the stars glimmering and quivering reflexly in the stream, and heard the whip-poor-wills whistling to their mates, and whip-poor-will notes echoing back again. We recalled the many incidents and unalloyed delights of both our trips, and were loth to realize that this was to be the last of our midsummer nights in our companionship with nature. With a touch of sentiment we yielded, finally, to the stillness and the calm, and, with our pipes whiffing their clouding odors about, mused and lapsed into the reveries of wayward fancy. The moon rose behind us. Its beams tipped the forest, over there, fronting us in grim silence, like an array of dark, weird, embattled phantoms, and their deep draperies of shadow vanished, and all the wood shone into shapes of golden light and beauty.

We lingered late and long, so as to enjoy the charm and glories of the summer night. The scene was about to change. All the way we had been free from shop. Even in sleep Queen Mab had not galloped her team of atomies over our lawyer fingers to make us straight dream of fees. But now that we were going back to shop, all shop, and shop at all times, was, perhaps, the dark thread in the weaving of our reveries. We made preparation for an early start by packing our luggage and paraphernalia for the last home portage, then to be laid aside, like armor taken off and hung up during the calm of peace.

Since the great fire of 1871, which, like a destroying angel, smote the forests of far-extending regions with a blast of flame, the lower twenty miles of the river are stripped of all woodland beauty. Burnt and blackened stems of branchless trees, without shade enough of foliage, except a rare small oasis of spreading green, to cover a camping party, with few and far between huts and cabins, mark with desolation this part of the route. For this reason, and from the burning glare of the sun, our descent of that day was the exceptional coursing of the voyage unattended with charm, comfort or pleasure. We had Dr. Andrews and party in sight a long way down the river, in the van of us. We overhauled him only at the head of the log-jam, three miles from Marinette and Menominee, where further passage was apparently blocked. He, with his sons, was sitting on the bank, at full stop, with his skiff at bay, in much perplexity.

There is no critical or delicate case of surgery that could confuse or bewilder the eminent surgeon, but here was a dilemma too much for all his science and skill. It was evidently to him a case like Mercutio's wound, "past all surgery." But our boys were equal to the emergency. As loggers and log-drivers, a chaos and muddle of floated pines were no novelty or hopeless dead-lock to them. They hopped and skipped from one undulatory and rolling log to another, far enough down to take in the situation. They started the logs afloat, and by degrees got those that barred our way deployed and going aspread, so that in the gaps opened we could make way and tide along with the floating mass. The doctor and his boat threaded through in our wake. The skiff was built by his own sons. In it they and he had cruised the river as high as Badwater, merely for a vacation tour, in search of the picturesque, to rough it, and to realize the hygiene of open air, of summer skies and of forest life.

We advanced along with the immense fleet of logs for nearly a mile, hemmed in sometimes in peril of a crush, like arctic boats in moving floes of ice. But at length the floating ceased. The logs began to compact immovably into a hopeless jam. We had nothing left us to do but to lift out and unload the canoe, and portage it and the equipage over the logs to shore, to be teamed thence a couple of miles to Marinette. Hot and glaring as was the day, the tramp was not formidable to us, then well used to footing distances, and we made our way on foot. In good season we shook off the dust of our feet at the Dunlap House, not inapt for a plentiful meal at the first tap of the dinner-gong.

*Cedant arma togæ.* Our vacation and our tour

were ended. From the wood in nature's unbroken luxuriance and repose, to the stir and whirl of city life; from the canoe, one of the earliest contrivances of primitive man for boating, to the Pullman palace-car, the latest and perfect scheme for easing, soothing and luxuriating travel; from the trivial fatigues of the portage to the serious burdens of daily toil;—these were our extreme transitions of a single day.

Three of us, lawyers, in the early August, wearied of labor, threw off the professional harness and sought freedom of action, rest, health and recreation—to have a good time. We knew where and how to find it, and we had found it in exuberance of satisfaction. We had left our library books to find more animating and living books in the running brooks, sermons in the stones and good in everything. Our outfit was simple, but enough, and not overburdensome in the canoe or on the portage. Our train of Indian attendants was more and better than we expected; all of them were ready and eager to do their utmost in their parts and sphere, and, as we believe, mutual attachments have entwined them and us as friends for all time. Our adieus with them were warm with the sincerity of friendliness.

And so, looking back over our excursion, in which could be recalled no single jar or discordance in the common fellowship of the party—without a growl or murmur of complaint, or even a physical pain or mishap to be remembered, the only regret being that of a too early severance or separation while on the route—we felt and were at peace of mind and rest of body, content with each other and ourselves. And all were ready to join in the spirit of the closing words of the fisher and hunter in good old Izaak Walton's book, "Let the blessing of St. Peter's master be mine and upon all that are lovers of virtue, and dare trust in his providence and be quiet and go a-angling."

## No. 1.

### DISTANCE TABLE.—BRULE RIVER.

| | | | TOTAL | From Republic |
|---|---|---|---|---|
| From | Lake Brule | | | |
| To | Hagerman, or Big Lake Portage | 8 | | |
| " | First Lake (Portage) | 1¼ | | |
| " | Hagerman Lake (Portage ¼ mile) | ½ | 1¾ | |
| " | Pickerel Lake (Portage ¼ mile) | 2¼ | 4 | |
| " | Big Hill, Portage | ½ | 8½ | |
| " | Foot Big Hill Portage (Portage 3½ miles) | 4 | 12½ | |
| " | Mouth Maple Creek | 17 | 29½ | |
| " | Lake Chicagon Portage | 3½ | 33 | 88 |
| " | Cedar Camp | 2½ | 35½ | 90½ |
| " | Little Brule Falls | 2½ | 38 | 93 |
| " | Boot Lakes Camp, (Chickabiddy) | 4½ | 42½ | 97½ |
| " | 1st Boot Lake (Portage) | ½ | | |
| " | 2d Lake (Portage, ¼ mile) | 1 | 1½ | |
| " | 3d Lake (Portage, ¾ mile) | 1¾ | 3¼ | |
| " | Pine River (Portage, 2¾ miles) | 3¼ | 6½ | |
| " | Brule Dam, (1878) | 1 | 43½ | 98½ |
| " | Armstrong's Camp | 1 | 44½ | 99½ |
| " | La Montaigne's Upper Camp | 2 | 46½ | 101½ |
| " | Cauldwell's (La Montaigne's Farm, ¾ miles) | 3 | 49½ | 104½ |
| " | R. Stephenson's, Brule Farm | 5 | 54½ | 109½ |
| " | Brule Falls (Mouth Paint River) | 1½ | 56 | 111 |
| " | Mouth Otter Creek | 2¾ | 58¾ | 113¾ |
| " | Mouth Brule River | 1¼ | 60 | 115 |

## No. 2.

### DISTANCE TABLE.—WAGON ROAD, QUINISECK TO BRULE RIVER. (1878)

| | | | TOTAL |
|---|---|---|---|
| From | Quiniseck | | |
| To | First Creek | 1¾ | |
| " | Second Creek | 2¾ | 4½ |
| " | Outlet Lake Antoine | 1½ | 6 |
| " | Bass Lake | ½ | 6½ |
| " | Twin Falls Bridge | 2 | 8½ |

WAGON ROAD, QUINISECK TO BRULE RIVER—*Continued.*

| | | | |
|---|---|---|---|
| To | Badwater Lakes | 5¾ | 14¼ |
| " | Commonwealth Mine | 3¼ | 17½ |
| " | Otter Creek (Outlet Fisher's Lake) | 1½ | 19 |
| " | Brule River (R. Stephenson's Brule Farm) | 3¼ | 22¼ |
| " Supply Road. | Two Lakes | 4½ | 26¾ |
| " Supply Road. | Armstrong's Camp | 3¼ | 30 |
| " Supply Road. | Brule Dam | 1¼ | 31¼ |

## No. 3.

## DISTANCE TABLE.—WAGON ROADS TO PIKE RIVER.

| | | | TOTAL |
|---|---|---|---|
| From | Section 18 (C. & N. W. Ry.) | | |
| To | Smith's Farm (mouth Little Cedar) | 1½ | |
| " | Relay House | 4 | 5½ |
| " | Little Shakey River | 5 | 10½ |
| " | Mouth Pike River (Ford) | 7½ | 18 |
| " Supply Road. | Half-way Creek | 6 | 24 |
| " Supply Road. | High Landings | 6 | 30 |
| " Supply Road. | Dave's Falls | 7½ | 37½ |
| " Supply Road. | Forks Dam | 1½ | 39 |
| From | Carney (Sec. 34½, C. & N. W. Ry.) | | |
| To | Little Cedar River | 4 | |
| " | N. Ludington Co.'s Pemerece Farm | 8 | 12 |
| " | Muscawana Creek | 5 | 17 |
| " | Little Muscawana Creek | 2¾ | 19¾ |
| " | Road to Forks of Pike | 3¼ | 23 |
| " Supply Road. | Caton Lakes | 2 | 25 |
| " Supply Road. | Fork's Pike River, (Pike Dam) | 4½ | 29½ |
| " Supply Road. | Dave's Falls | 1½ | 31 |
| " | North Branch Bridge | 8 | 31 |

## No. 4.

## DISTANCE TABLE.—MICHIGAMI RIVER.

| | | | TOTAL | From Republic |
|---|---|---|---|---|
| From | Michigammi | | | |
| To | Outlet, Lake Michigami (Portage, one mile left bank) | 7 | | |

MICHIGAMI RIVER—*Continued.*

| | | | | |
|---|---|---|---|---|
| To | Republic | 11 | 18 | |
| " | Foot Long Rapids (Portage 2 miles, right bank) | 14½ | 32½ | 14½ |
| " | Floodwood Portage (Portage ⅛ mile, left bank) | 8½ | 41 | 23 |
| " | Lake Ellen | 8 | 49 | 31 |
| " | Fence, or Mitchigan River | 4½ | 5[illegible]½ | 35½ |
| " | Deer River | 4½ | 58 | 40 |
| " | Upper Michigami Falls (Portage ⅛ mile, right bank) | 4 | 62 | 44 |
| " | Lake Mary, Portage | 9 | 71 | 53 |
| " | Little Norway Portage (Po tage ⅛ mile, left bank) | 5 | 76 | 58 |
| " | Big Falls, or Grand Portage (Portage 1½ miles, left bank) | 6 | 82 | 64 |
| " | Mouth Michigami River (Portage at Falls ⅛ miles, right bank | 8 | 90 | 72 |

## No. 5.

### DISTANCE TABLE.—MICHIGAMI RIVER TO BRULE RIVER, VIA LAKE MARY AND PAINT RIVER.

| | | | TOTAL | From Republic |
|---|---|---|---|---|
| From | Michigami River | | | |
| To | Lake Mary | ¼ | - | 53¼ |
| " | Deer Fence Portage | 1½ | 1¾ | 54¾ |
| " | Paint River (Portage) | 2 | 3¾ | 56¾ |
| " | Crystal, or Paint Falls | 6½ | 10¼ | 63¼ |
| " | Mouth Sugar, or Trout River | 8½ | 18¾ | 71¾ |
| " | Sugar River, Portage | 2½ | 21¼ | 74¼ |
| " | Mud Lake (Portage) | ½ | 21¾ | 74¾ |
| " | Sugar River (Portage, 1½ miles) | 1¾ | 23½ | 76½ |
| " | Lone Grave, or Bass Lake | 2½ | 26 | 79 |
| " | Foot Lake Chicagon | 3¾ | 29¾ | 82¾ |
| " | Head Lake Chicagon | 3½ | 33¼ | 86¼ |
| " | Lake Minnie (Portage) | ½ | 33¾ | 86¾ |
| " | Brule River (Portage, ¾ mile) | 1¼ | 35 | 88 |

## No. 6.
## DISTANCE TABLE.—MENOMINEE RIVER.

| From | | | TOTAL | From Republic |
|---|---|---|---|---|
| From To | Mouths Michigami & Brule Rivers | | | |
| " | Badwater (Indian Village)....... | 6½ | | 121½ |
| " | Badwater Crossing (Ferry)...... | 2 | 8½ | 123½ |
| " | Upper Twin Falls (Portage, left bank)..................... | 2¼ | 10¾ | 125¾ |
| " | Lower Twin Falls (Portage, left bank)..... ................ | ½ | 11¼ | 126¼ |
| " | Mouth Pine River............... | 4½ | 15¾ | 130¾ |
| " | Head Quiniseck Rapids, { Long Portage, 1¾ miles, left bank. 2 Short Portages. ¾ miles, left bank........ | 6½ | 22¼ | 137¼ |
| " | Upper, or Big Quiniseck Falls (Portage, left bank)......... | 1¾ | 24 | 139 |
| " | Lower, or Little Quiniseck Falls (Portage, left bank)......... | 4¾ | 28¾ | 143¾ |
| " | Head Sand Portage, { Long Portage, 2 miles, left bank. 2 Short Portages, ½ mile left bank............ | 1¾ | 32¼ | 174¼ |
| " | Foot Sand Portage.............. | 1¾ | 32¼ | 147¼ |
| " | New York Farm (Mouth Sturgeon River).................... | 4¼ | 36½ | 151½ |
| " | Sturgeon Falls (Portage, left bank) | 1 | 37½ | 152½ |
| " | Grand Island................... | 9 | 46½ | 161½ |
| " | "No Speak".................... | 2 | 48½ | 163½ |
| " | Pemeneebunwan Rapids (Portage, right bank)................ | ¾ | 49¼ | 164¼ |
| " | Pemeneebunwun Creek.......... | 2¾ | 52 | 167 |
| " | Pemenee Falls (Portage, right bank) ..................... | 2¾ | 54¾ | 169¾ |
| " | Pemenee Creek................. | ½ | 55¼ | 170¼ |
| " | N. L. Co.'s Pemenee Farm...... | 1 | 56¼ | 171¼ |
| " | Muscawana (Indian Village)..... | 2¾ | 59 | 174 |
| " | Muscawana Island.............. | ½ | 59½ | 174½ |
| " | Muscawana Rapids............. | 1¾ | 61¼ | 176¼ |
| " | Chalk Hill Rapids.............. | 1¾ | 63 | 178 |
| " | White Rapids.................. | 4½ | 67½ | 182½ |
| " | White Rapids (Indian Village)... | ¾ | 68¼ | 183¼ |
| " | Sixty Islands.................. | ½ | 68¾ | 183¾ |
| " | Mouth Pike River.............. | 3 | 71¾ | 186¾ |

MENOMINEE RIVER—*Continued.*

| | | | | |
|---|---|---|---|---|
| To | K. C. Co.'s Pike Farm......... | 1½ | 73¼ | 188¼ |
| " | Mouth Shakey River ........... | 1 | 74¼ | 189¼ |
| " | Head Wausauka Portage (Portage ⅛ mile, left bank)........... | 4¼ | 78½ | 193½ |
| " | Foot Wausauka Portage (Portage ⅛ mile, left bank)........... | 3½ | 82 | 197 |
| " | Pock Du Nock................... | 4½ | 86½ | 201½ |
| " | Head Long Reach... ........... | 5¾ | 92¼ | 207¼ |
| " | Relay House.................... | 4 | 96¼ | 211¼ |
| " | Head Grand Rapids............. | ½ | 96¾ | 211¾ |
| " | Foot Grand Rapids, (Mouth Little Cedar River)................. | 3¾ | 100½ | 215½ |
| " | Twin Islands................... | 6¼ | 106¾ | 221¾ |
| " | Twin Creek..................... | 6½ | 113¼ | 228¼ |
| " | Little River..................... | 6¾ | 120 | 235 |
| " | Upper Dam...................... | 1½ | 121½ | 236½ |
| " | Mouth Menominee River........ | 3½ | 125 | 240 |

www.ingramcontent.com/pod-product-compliance
Lightning Source LLC
Chambersburg PA
CBHW032057220426
43664CB00008B/1032